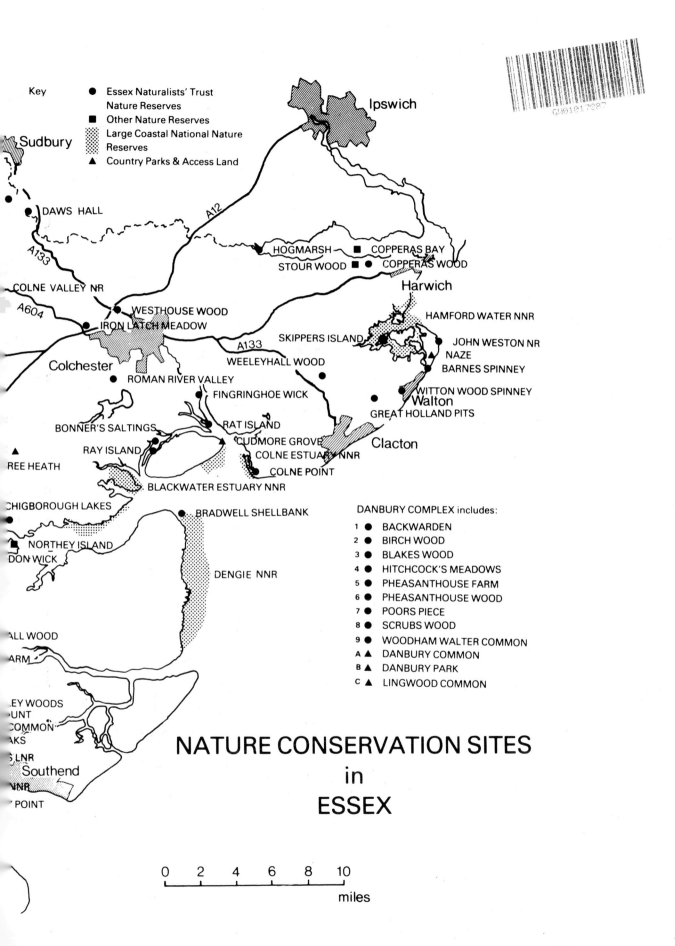

Key
● Essex Naturalists' Trust Nature Reserves
■ Other Nature Reserves
░ Large Coastal National Nature Reserves
▲ Country Parks & Access Land

Sudbury

● DAWS HALL

A12

A133

HOGMARSH — ■ COPPERAS BAY
STOUR WOOD ■ ● COPPERAS WOOD

Harwich

COLNE VALLEY NR

A604

WESTHOUSE WOOD
IRON LATCH MEADOW

HAMFORD WATER NNR

SKIPPERS ISLAND

A133

JOHN WESTON NR
NAZE
BARNES SPINNEY

WEELEYHALL WOOD

Colchester

● ROMAN RIVER VALLEY

WITTON WOOD SPINNEY
Walton
GREAT HOLLAND PITS

● FINGRINGHOE WICK

BONNER'S SALTINGS

RAT ISLAND

CUDMORE GROVE
COLNE ESTUARY NNR

Clacton

RAY ISLAND

▲
REE HEATH

COLNE POINT

BLACKWATER ESTUARY NNR

CHIGBOROUGH LAKES

● BRADWELL SHELLBANK

■ NORTHEY ISLAND
DON WICK

DENGIE NNR

DANBURY COMPLEX includes:
1 ● BACKWARDEN
2 ● BIRCH WOOD
3 ● BLAKES WOOD
4 ● HITCHCOCK'S MEADOWS
5 ● PHEASANTHOUSE FARM
6 ● PHEASANTHOUSE WOOD
7 ● POORS PIECE
8 ● SCRUBS WOOD
9 ● WOODHAM WALTER COMMON
A ▲ DANBURY COMMON
B ▲ DANBURY PARK
C ▲ LINGWOOD COMMON

ALL WOOD
ARM

EY WOODS
UNT
COMMON
AKS

LNR
Southend
NNR
POINT

NATURE CONSERVATION SITES
in
ESSEX

0 2 4 6 8 10

miles

THE NATURE OF ESSEX

Dunlin and Thames sailing barge. (RH)

OVER: Brent Geese and shelduck at the edge of the saltmarsh in Hamford
Water. (AH)

THE NATURE OF ESSEX

THE WILDLIFE AND ECOLOGY
OF THE COUNTY

BY

DAVID CORKE

with Paintings by

ALAN HARRIS

Drawings by

CLAIRE APPLEBY, JOANNA FOLEY,
MARK HANSON AND RICHARD HULL

and Photographs by
TED BENTON, DAVID CORKE, BOB GLOVER,
MARTIN GREGORY, DON HUNFORD, STEPHEN LONG,
H. McSWEENEY, TERRY ILLSLEY AND LEWIS WOODWARD

Published with the co-operation and in aid of
THE ESSEX NATURALISTS' TRUST

FOREWORD BY THE RT HON LORD BUXTON, MC DL

BARRACUDA BOOKS LIMITED
BUCKINGHAM, ENGLAND
MCMLXXXIV

THE NATURE OF BRITAIN SERIES

PUBLISHED BY BARRACUDA BOOKS LIMITED,
BUCKINGHAM, ENGLAND
IN THIS SECOND EDITION, 1986
AND PRINTED BY
BUSIPRINT LIMITED,
BUCKINGHAM, ENGLAND
BOUND BY
GREEN STREET BINDERY LIMITED,
OXFORD, ENGLAND

COLOUR PLATES AND JACKET
PRINTED BY
CHENEY & SONS LIMITED,
BANBURY, OXON

COLOUR LITHOGRAPHY BY
GATEWAY PLATEMAKERS LIMITED,
LONDON, ENGLAND

LITHOGRAPHY BY
MRM GRAPHICS LIMITED,
WINSLOW, ENGLAND

DISPLAY SET IN BASKERVILLE AND
TEXT SET IN 10½/12pt BASKERVILLE BY
BEDFORDSHIRE GRAPHICS LIMITED,
BEDFORD, ENGLAND

© Essex Naturalists' Trust

ISBN 0 86023 267 0

Contents

List of Colour Plates

Essex is NOT flat and uninteresting; Essex is slightly undulating and uninteresting.

Anon: quoted by A.C. Edwards in his *History of Essex,* 1978.

Essex did not always lie in the shadow of London smoke. There was a time, before tourist days, when it shone out in wealth and dignity among the regions of England.

A.R. Hope Montcrieff in his *Essex,* 1909.

Essex is not as popular a touring and sight-seeing county as it deserves to be. People say that is due to the squalor of Liverpool Street Station.

Nikolaus Pevsner, *Essex,* 1954.

Essex is a large square with two sides water. It is a stronger contrast of beauty and ugliness than any other southern English county.

John Betjeman, *Parish Churches of England and Wales,* 1980.

Foreword

by Lord Buxton, MC, DL

Nothing could be more rewarding for me than to contribute to this exceptional book, because all my life the wildlife habitat of Essex and especially its birds, have been a passionate interest of mine. Fifty years ago during school holidays I spent all the daylight hours, usually on my bike, in Epping Forest, where the dark fallow deer were then numerous; or watching redshank and snipe by the River Roding; or in Wanstead Park to see the heronry; or on the coast at Mersea and Old Hall Marshes watching wildfowl or short-eared owls or, when I could get away with it, in the sewage farm near my home, where there were reed buntings and sedge warblers and many others, after which my mother used to have me hosed down in the yard before I was allowed back into the house.

Since then the wildlife threshold in Essex seems to have improved in many respects, mainly because of the vigorous momentum stimulated and sustained by conservationist bodies and especially by the Essex Naturalists' Trust. The steady establishment of more and more reserves and sanctuaries is manifestation of the deep and traditional desire of people in Essex to preserve their heritage and especially to conserve wild habitat. It is naturally gratifying that David Corke refers so generously to the part my family played in saving Essex forests, and it is a source of much satisfaction to me that my own small reserve of woodland and ponds now belongs to the Essex Naturalists' Trust. After more than half a century it is hardly surprising therefore that I am proud to be associated with *Nature of Essex,* which I consider a landmark in the history of the county.

After reading this book, especially the early chapters on the background and origins, one will be able to travel round the varied landscapes and seascapes of Essex with a new interest and a new understanding. The wonderfully lucid account of the origins of saltmarsh and shingle, mudflats and estuaries, is an education in itself. Nobody can fail to profit by it, and most will probably read it all time and again. The illustrations will be a source of constant pleasure.

This is the Silver Jubilee of the Trust, and this brilliant work will provide just the spur that its impressive membership of eleven thousand needs. Congratulations to all on the Jubilee, and congratulations to the author and the whole team concerned with the production of this masterpiece.

Brent geese fly V-formation over the Blackwater estuary. (RG)

Introduction

Tradition dictates that the last thing an author does before delivering his book to the publisher is to write the introduction. The publisher then puts it at the front of the book in the belief that it will convince the bookshop browser that he cannot afford to be without the book — despite the fact that the author will have used the introduction to apologise for all the book's shortcomings!

So why should you buy *The Nature of Essex?* I have tried to make the book serve three different functions. First, it is a picture book to look at and enjoy. It will show you some of the Essex wildlife and countryside that you may not yet have seen in real life. Since you will have flipped through the book before reading the introduction, you will already have seen the beautiful paintings, drawings and photographs which so many people have generously made available for this book. The individual artists and photographers are acknowledged in the captions to their work. The Cambridge University Committee for Aerial Photography and the Royal Aircraft Establishment were extremely helpful in searching out suitable aerial and satellite photographs. The Passmore Edwards Museum provided excellent black and white prints of those photographs where the original was a colour transparency.

Second, it is a book to read. Each chapter takes a particular habitat and tries to explain how the interactions of man and nature have produced the Essex countryside we see today. There is some logic to the sequence of chapters: starting at the sea, we work towards the City. This sequence is, roughly, from the most natural to the most artificial habitats. Each chapter is meant to be a complete story which will make sense in isolation from the rest of the book.

Finally, I hope the book can be used as a work of reference which will lead you to more detailed sources of information. Most of what I have written is based on published information. I suspect that Essex must be amongst the best studied of all counties: the books and journals to which I have referred occupy many yards of shelf. My debt to the authors of all these works is enormous — and I have failed to acknowledge it by proper references in the text. My excuse is that the individual chapters are meant to be easy reading — not broken-up with references, foot-notes and scientific names. The appendices will, I hope, provide an adequate guide to my main sources of reference, indices to scientific names and a guide to the many areas of conservation importance. I make no excuse for including some statistical information in the text. I enjoy such facts and figures and they may be of use to students preparing their school projects!

The Nature Conservancy Council, Anglian Water Authority, Thames Water Authority and Lee Valley Regional Park have produced helpful answers to many questions. The Essex Naturalists' Trust encouraged me to start work on the book and have been very helpful in providing information and checking early drafts. Especial thanks for detailed comments on the draft are due to Bill Butcher, Laurie Forsyth and Geoff Pyman. Despite all this help, I do not doubt that many errors remain. For these I take full responsibility — I would be very grateful for corrections from all who notice errors so that a future edition can amend them.

The opinions expressed in this book are my own. They are not necessarily the official views of the Essex Naturalists' Trust.

The Essex Naturalists' Trust, whose silver jubilee this book celebrates, is honoured by the Foreword kindly written by Lord Buxton, who has long been active in his support of the Trust.

DAVID CORKE
Wimbish, Essex
July 1984.

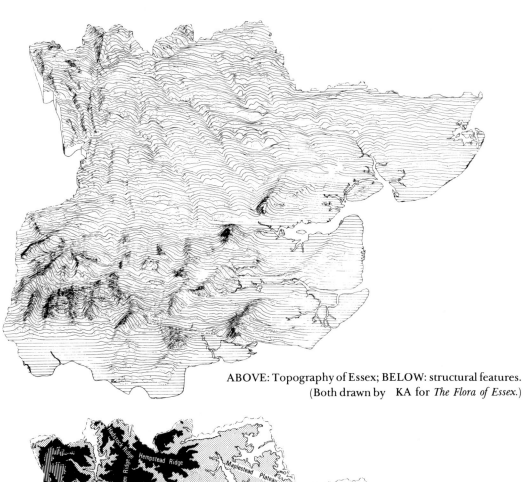

ABOVE: Topography of Essex; BELOW: structural features.
(Both drawn by   KA for *The Flora of Essex.*)

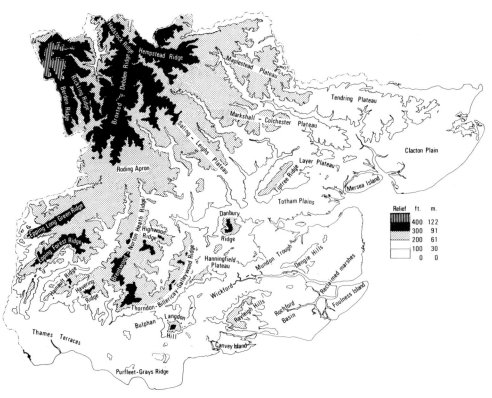

Relief	ft.	m.
	400	122
	300	91
	200	61
	100	30
	0	0

12

Background and Origins

Fallow deer in a medieval Essex forest. (JF)

Essex is a county almost entirely bounded by water. To the east is the sea, to the south the Thames, on the west the Lea and to the north the Stour. Only in the extreme north-west is the county boundary not a waterway.

These natural borders of the geographical county have, through most of the long history of Essex, also been the political boundaries. Before the Roman invasion, the Lea Valley marked the border between the warlike (Hertfordshire) Belgae and the more peaceful (Essex) Trinovantes. After the Romans, Essex became a kingdom and obtained its name: the kingdom of the East Saxons. Later still, the Danish invasions brought the Danelaw to eastern England and, in 886, the River Lea became the frontier between the Danes and the English.

Almost all the boundaries of the old kingdom of Essex remain the boundaries of the present-day county. The main exception is in the south-west, where rapidly expanding London has repeatedly swallowed up parts of Essex. The most recent bite was in 1964, when the Greater London Council was created and consumed 18 former Essex parishes.

This book is concerned more with the natural history than the human history of Essex. Over the centuries, generations of naturalists have made Essex one of the best studied of all English counties. The 1974 *Flora of Essex* and the 1984 *New Guide to the Birds of Essex* typify the excellence of natural history survey work in the county. In these, and all other recent surveys, naturalists have continued to use the old, geographical county as their recording unit. This helps make modern surveys directly comparable with records from the many studies carried out in Victorian times. This book continues the tradition. Whenever 'Essex' is mentioned, unless it is explicitly stated otherwise, the area referred to is the administrative county of Essex plus the London Boroughs of Barking, Havering, Redbridge, Newham and Waltham Forest. This area is almost precisely that covered by the two 'biological' vice-counties of north and south Essex, used for biological recording since 1852.

Defined in this way, Essex has an area of 3957 sq km (1529 sq miles): and it is one of the larger English counties. It also has an almost incredibly high human population: just over two and a half million at the last count. This gives a population density of 637 people per sq km (1648 per sq mile). If the old 'kingdom' of Essex had retained its independence, it would rank as far and away the most densely populated country in western Europe, with a density 65% above that of the Netherlands.

Even on a worldwide basis, Essex is one of the most overpopulated regions. There are only four countries with a higher population density than Essex — all four are tiny island 'city-states' whose combined surface area is less than half that of Essex. They are Bermuda, Malta, Singapore and

Hong Kong. When, early in the 19th century, the population of Essex was one tenth of its present level, the population density was about the same as present-day China. Nine hundred years ago, at the time of the Domesday survey, there was one person for every 160 crowded into present day Essex.

Perhaps we should remember these figures before being too critical of third-world countries' conservation problems associated with 'over-population'. Perhaps, too, there is some comfort in these statistics. The remaining chapters of this book will make it clear that, although much changed by man, the county of Essex still contains a rich diversity of semi-natural habitats. It is still possible to walk remote areas of Essex and enjoy the presence of wildlife and absence of people. So, maybe, we should not be quite so pessimistic about the survival of wildlife in other, less populated parts of the world. On the other hand, Essex wildlife has suffered badly. Only counting those species known to have bred in the county, we have lost about a third of our species of land mammals and butterflies and 10% of our birds and flowering plants.

Most books about Essex start by explaining that, although everyone thinks of Essex as a flat county, it really is not all that flat. Much of the county can be described as gently rolling countryside, dissected by many river valleys. At its height, in the extreme north-west, chalk hills rise to over 120m (400 ft). But, in truth, Essex is flat and low-lying. Its most important wildlife habitats are the huge expanses of coastal mudflats, estuaries and saltmarshes. Inland, Essex is certainly not as flat and featureless as the fenlands of Cambridgeshire, nor most of the rest of East Anglia. But compared with most of Britain, it has less steep slopes, less high ground, and no outcrops of ancient rocks. Essex would not have presented our ancestors with many surprises when they migrated from the Low Countries to England.

In climate, too, Essex resembles the adjacent continent more than the norm for Britain as a whole. Compared with most of the rest of England, Essex has a low rainfall, more sunshine, higher summer temperatures and lower winter ones — a true 'continental' climate.

The coastal regions of Essex are the only large areas of the country to get less than 500mm (20 in) of rain a year. Over the whole county, the average is about 600mm (24 in). Unusually, most of this rain falls in summer, only 44% falling between October and March. In the rest of England, most rain falls in winter. The clay soils of Essex retain moisture effectively, so the low rainfall has little adverse effect on most plant-life. Indeed, the warm summers make Essex one of the most productive arable areas of Britain. On the other hand, Essex has the lowest humidity of any English county and it may be this factor that explains the rather restricted range of ferns, mosses and liverworts.

The Essex coast shares with the seaside resorts of the south coast the distinction of being the only parts of England with a daily average of more than 4½ hours of sunshine. Inland the average is between 4 and 4½, the same as most of southern England. The average July temperature in southern Essex is over 17°C, the highest average in Britain. The winter average of about 4°C is obviously not as low as the high ground and far north of England but is cold compared with most of southern and western England — where the warming effects of the Gulf stream moderate the winter climate. Probably the most important point about the Essex winter is not the average temperature but the fact that, in normal years, periods of sharp frost alternate rapidly with quite mild spells. This pattern of weather is responsible for breaking up the heavy clay into a fine tilth.

There is one part of Essex, the metropolitan area, where winter temperatures are much higher than normal Essex figures. On a cold winter's day, London areas can be 6°C above that of rural Essex. Through the whole winter, heat loss from human homes keeps the urban areas 1.4°C above the rural temperature. It may be to claim this central heating benefit, that vast flocks of starlings move into town each night, to roost many miles from their rural and suburban feeding grounds.

The explanation for the generally flat nature of Essex is the relative youth of the county's underlying rocks. The rocks that make the spectacular scenery of the west country were already old when the dinosaurs ruled the earth. At that time the chalks, clays and gravels of Essex were still in the process of formation.

One hundred million years ago, in the Cretaceous period, which ended in the death of the dinosaurs, the continental plate carrying Europe was pulling away from America and creating the Atlantic ocean. The bit of Europe which was to become Britain was at the bottom of a warm sea and further south than its present day position: about as far south as present day Spain. 'Essex' was well out to sea and did not receive much sediment washed from nearby land. The Chalk Sea must have been incredibly clear. Abundant algae and protozoa extracted calcium carbonate from the

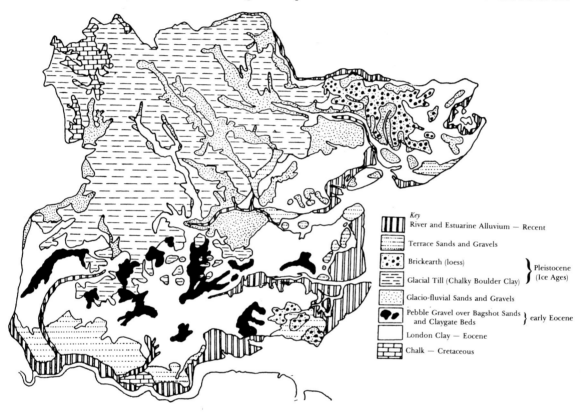

A simplified geological map of Essex. (RA)

water, made it into shells around their bodies and, when they died, sank down to form pure deposits of chalk several hundred metres thick. Much later, this chalk was lifted up and became the surface of 'Essex' and was considerably eroded. Today there are between two and three hundred metres of chalk underlying the whole of Essex, although over most of the county the chalk is well hidden, buried under a couple of hundred metres of later deposits of clays and gravels.

Only in two parts of Essex, at opposite ends of the county, is chalk exposed at or near the surface. In the extreme north-west, the very end of the Chiltern Hills reach just over the county boundary. The headwaters of the rivers Cam and Stort also cut into the Essex 'highlands' and

15

expose the chalk on their valley sides. In the Grays area of south Essex, what is really part of the North Downs system occurs on the Essex side of the Thames. Here, as well as in the northern chalk areas, man has mined chalk from many huge chalk pits. These old chalk quarries provide habitats for the richest variety of chalk loving plants in Essex.

Fifty million years ago the chalk surface of Essex returned to a submarine existence, this time in shallow, murky, coastal seas: the continental plate carrying England had drifted further north. Coastal seas receive a rain of sediment from the rivers flowing into them. Inshore, the heavier particles deposit quickest and form sands. The Thanet Sands, visible in the chalkpits of the Grays area, were formed at this time. Later, and more important, the sea deepened and the rain of particles became finer. They eventually formed the 270 metres of London Clay that now cover the chalk across most of southern Essex.

At the end of the period of London Clay formation, the sea shallowed and sands were again deposited. These Claygate and Bagshot Beds are now sandy caps on top of the London Clay in several parts of south Essex: in the Brentwood, Billericay and Mill Green areas, for example. These sands offer easy digging and a study of the distribution of badger setts has shown that they are more likely to be found in these geological regions than elsewhere in Essex. Unfortunately, Claygate and Bagshot Beds are easy digging for humans too, and the recent, massive increase in illegal badger digging has destroyed many of the setts in what was once the badger's Essex headquarters.

Ten million years ago the earth movements that created the Alps also, rather less spectacularly, lifted Essex back up above sea-level. At first it would have been a plain of London Clay. The north-west was then, as it is now, higher than the rest of Essex and the London Clay eroded away, eventually exposing the chalk. This went on for nine million years. Judging by fossils elsewhere in the world, there was probably a rich and varied fauna of large mammals, of species not now in existence anywhere. There are hardly any fossils from this period to tell us in detail about Essex. From a later period, the abundant fossils in the red crag of the Naze cliffs give a good indication of the animal life of coastal Essex just before the ice ages. The climate got colder and the animal life was swept away by the ice cap advancing south. The scene was set for the most recent geological upheaval to shape the face of Essex.

The ice ages of the Pleistocene period were separated by warm periods, when Essex developed a flora and fauna as rich and exciting as the best of the national parks in Africa. But at the height of the glaciations Essex would have resembled the high arctic: ice cap and glaciers with a little tundra vegetation in the extreme south.

The most recent glaciation ended only ten thousand years ago, after three thousand years of warmer weather and a melting ice cap. The ice cap was not just ice; within it was a glorious mixture of fragmented chalk, flints, shales, clay and plenty of quite large boulders. The melting ice cap deposited all this on the underlying chalk and London clay. These glacial soils are the chalky boulder clays of Essex and the southern boundary of the boulder clay on the geological map is the southern limit of the ice age glaciation.

Under the boulder clay is a gravel layer, also of glacial origin, and the rivers that cut through the boulder clay regions expose this gravel on the valley sides. The extensive areas of gravels and sands along the Lea Valley and western part of the Thames were deposited after the ice age, carried by wide rivers flooded with melt water from the glaciers. These rivers had wide flood-plains and terraces. Where the water flowed fast, gravels would be deposited. Glacial outwash sands and gravels lie close to the surface over much of north-east Essex well to the east of the boulder clay limit. A wide, slow-flowing river, flooding out over its flat terraces on either side, would leave a finer soil. These alluvial soils would have covered much of the flat plain across what is now the North Sea. When it was dry the soil would be blown inland and collect in valleys where it remains today — the brickearths of the Southend area and to the north of Colchester.

The most recent deposits of silt have created the alluvial plains beside rivers flowing on their present courses. Other silt has been trapped by saltmarshes growing out into the estuary.

At the height of the last glaciation there can have been little wildlife. Most of Essex was ice cap and the rest would have been the most extreme form of tundra: a few heathers, dwarf shrubs and some lemmings perhaps. This means that all the present day wildlife of Essex has arrived during the twelve thousand or so years since the ice began to retreat.

At the end of the ice age, Britain was not an island. The Thames flowed across a low lying plain in what is now the southern part of the North Sea. It probably merged with the Rhine before finally discharging into the sea. So, as the climate improved, both plants and animals could colonise across from Europe, into southern England. At first Essex would have been covered with birch and pine forests. By about 7,500 years ago the climate was quite similar to the present one; there had been time for deciduous forests to develop and all our native wildlife had arrived. A little before this time, the melting ice cap, rapidly receding northwards towards its present position, had caused a considerable rise in sea level. The low lying plains were flooded, the North Sea joined the English Channel and Britain was an island. The sea flooded parts of the old, broad, Essex valleys, creating our present estuaries. The rivers, no longer swollen with melt water, shrank to their present sizes.

Stone Age man was already present in Essex but had, at this stage, made little impact on the natural environment. So the Essex of 7,500 to 5,000 years ago represented the true 'Nature of Essex' — and what it would be like today, had man not imposed his alterations on the landscape. The dry land was covered with a mixed woodland — the 'wildwood' containing small-leaved lime, oak, hazel, elm, pine, beech, ash, birch and hornbeam — roughly in that order of importance, although the proportions would have varied from place to place.

The rivers, in their lower reaches, were wide and shallow with extensive floodplains on either side. These would have been reedy swamps and open, wet grassy areas grading slowly through sallow and alder woods to the true wildwood on the higher ground. In the estuaries there would have been a similar transition from saltmarsh to woodland. The path to the Geedon Bay bird hide at Fingringhoe Wick nature reserve goes through a present day version of such a transition.

The wildlife that lives in the semi-natural environments, created by man from the natural scene of 5,000 years ago, is the subject of most of the rest of this book. Man has added many species, by accidental or deliberate introduction, to the list of Essex flora and fauna. Over the same period, man has exterminated many native species.

Dunlin and Thames sailing barge. (RH)

17

How the Lea Valley would have appeared in its natural state around 3000BC. The river meanders in a wide flood-plain with reed-beds and shallow pools in which spoonbills feed. (Spoonbills nested in the London area until the 16th century.) A red kite glides overhead (red kites bred commonly in Essex until the early 19th century). A beaver is gnawing an alder tree. (Beavers were hunted to extinction in Anglo-Saxon times.) A brown bear is walking towards the river to catch fish. (Brown bears were exterminated from all Britain before the Norman conquest.) A wild boar has come down from the Epping Forest ridge to drink. (Wild boar survived into medieval times.) A polecat searches for frogs on a shingle spit at the river edge. (Polecats were exterminated by gamekeepers in Victorian times.) An otter has climbed on to a fallen tree with a fish it has captured. (Otters died out in Essex during the 1960s and 1970s.) (AH)

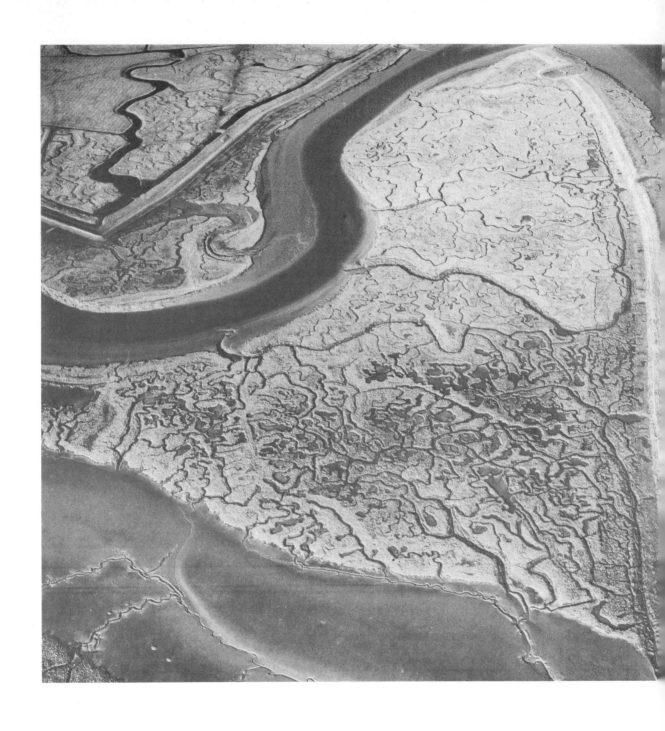

An aerial view of saltmarsh at the mouth of Hamford Water reveals the
complex pattern of creeks and saltpans. (UCCFAP)

Saltmarsh and Shingle

Yellow-horned poppies on a shingle-spit. (JF)

To the seaward side of the seawall, the saltmarshes and shingle banks are the most 'natural' of all Essex wildlife habitats. Both are constantly changing in their detailed geography, and yet they are still shaped by the interplay of the same natural forces that have always maintained them. They are the only above water habitats that neither need nor get management by man to maintain their mixture of plant and animal species. They are the natural 'climax' habitats of the Essex coast.

Like all coastal habitats, saltmarshes are zoned, with bands containing different species of plants at different levels of the tidal range. Because saltmarshes develop in sheltered areas and slope gently towards the sea, the zonation may be stretched out across a horizontal distance of over a kilometre. The vertical drop from the landward to seaward edge of the marsh is only one or two metres.

The seaward edge of the marsh is usually close to the level of high neap tides. At this level, the mud is covered twice each day by high tide and remains as mudflat. Each high tide brings in tiny particles of mud suspended in the water; these are deposited on the mud flat at the slack period around high tide. Provided the area is sheltered at the top of a wide mudflat, in an estuary, or behind a shingle spit, the outgoing tide does not wash deposits of mud away as fast as they are brought in: and so the mudflat slowly increases in height.

In the zone which is covered by the tide on only some days each month (the spring high tides), salt-tolerant land plants can get rooted and the saltmarsh starts to develop. The plants themselves slow down the tidal flow and hold mud particles better. So the saltmarsh goes on growing in height until it reaches the level at which it is only inundated a few times a year, at extreme high spring tides or during storms.

The process of saltmarsh development should result in new land being won from the sea in any suitably sheltered area of coast. In practice this does not always happen. There are two reasons. First, currents can change and cause the sea to erode away the saltmarsh as it floods up and down the saltmarsh creeks. Second, Essex is sinking into the sea! When the end of the ice age took the weight of the ice cap off western and northern Britain, the west coast started rising out of the sea. As Britain tips up, the east coast sinks by a corresponding amount. The rate of sinking is slow, around four metres since Roman times, but it is fast enough to explain why seawalls are raised higher and the Thames barrage built to protect London from flooding.

There are three major zones on most Essex saltmarshes: the low, mid and high marsh. Originally the high marsh would have graded into freshwater marsh, reed beds and then woodland. Now the seawall provides a sharp transition at the landward edge of the marsh.

The important colonisers which create the low marsh are common cord-grass, common saltmarsh grass, common glasswort, annual sea-blight and sea-aster. Common cord-grass has a particularly interesting history: it is a new species which has only existed since 1892. A related species, cord-grass proper, is the native species on British saltmarshes. An American species, smooth cord-grass, was introduced on the south coast in the early part of the last century. It hybridised with the native species, producing a sterile hybrid, which in turn underwent some complex genetic changes increasing its chromosome number and became a new, self-perpetuating species.

The new species was particularly vigorous and soon spread along the Hampshire and Sussex coast. It was so good at stabilising mudflats that it was introduced elsewhere. Between 1924 and 1933 thousands of cuttings of common cord-grass were planted along the Essex coast: the planting programme was grant-aided by the Ministry of Agriculture. This is probably the first, and far from the last, example of MAFF grants interfering with the ecology of Essex! The invading common-cord grass was so successful that the native cord-grass is now quite rare. It is still found on the Foulness and Maplin Sands: indeed this is the most important site for the grass in Britain.

The mid-marsh has a much greater diversity of plants: sea arrow-grass, sea purslane, sea plantain and perennial glasswort, for example. There are several other glassworts, each with its own special requirements and region of the marsh. The plants that give the mid-marsh its beauty are thrift and sea lavender. Thrift is also called sea-pink and its deep pink flowers colour the early summer marsh, giving way in high summer to the violet-blue flowers of the sea lavender. The sea purslane is one of the commonest plants and spreads up on to the high saltmarsh, where it is joined by sea wormwood and shrubby sea-blight.

It should be obvious from the fact that nearly every saltmarsh plant is called 'sea' something or other, that saltmarshes demand special adaptations of the plants that live there: they can then live nowhere else but the shore.

The main problem, a little surprisingly, is lack of water. Saltmarsh soil is constantly wet with saltwater, and the plants of the lower marsh are covered by high tide for two or three hours on some days. Sea-water is such a concentrated salt solution that it draws water out of most normal plants and causes them to wilt. So saltmarsh plants need special adaptations which allow their roots to pump water in, against the natural tendency for it to be drawn out by osmosis. The plants may have a higher concentration of salt in them than normal species, but not as high as the sea-water. Many saltmarsh plants, sea lavender for example, have special salt glands on the surface of their leaves that can get rid of surplus salt.

Getting dilute water inside the plant costs it a lot of energy: water is precious just as it is for desert plants, and so it is not so surprising that some saltmarsh plants have similar adaptations to those in deserts. The glassworts store water in succulent green stems and sea purslane has its leaves coated with tiny scales that reduce the rate of water loss.

Saltmarshes are not completely covered by plants. A detailed study of part of the marsh at Colne Point nature reserve showed that a quarter of the area consisted of muddy creeks. From the air these creeks look like a miniature version of a river system. Unlike rivers, where the water always flows one way, the tide floods up the creeks and then the water drains back on the ebb. So the pattern of erosion is not quite the same as that formed in a true river.

If the creeks are the saltmarsh river system, then the saltpans are its lakes. Saltpans may originate by being cut off from bends in creeks or by natural depressions in the saltmarsh becoming filled by the sea at very high tides. In hot weather saltpans dry out and the salt crystallises on the bottom; but in periods of heavy rainfall the rain dilutes the water in the pans and they become much nearer to fresh than salt water. So the animal life in saltpans needs to be exceptionally tolerant of varying salt concentrations. Most of the larger saltpans in Essex have common gobies and shore crabs as well as a limited variety of smaller crustaceans.

Saltmarsh vegetation, although it has to adapt to the problems of saltmarsh life, benefits from the fertility of saltmarsh soils. Each year the new growth on an area of saltmarsh can equal or exceed the plant growth in the same area of woodland or farm field. Most of this massive plant production decays and is used by marine organisms in the saltmarsh mud, or is washed out into the estuary and used there. There is a limited range of land animals that specialise in feeding within the saltmarsh, but this includes some particularly interesting birds and moths.

Many small, sparrow-sized birds move across saltmarshes in winter, feeding on seeds of the saltmarsh plants. The twite, a winter visitor to Essex, is virtually restricted to this habitat. Another winter visitor is the rock pipit, a species for which there is no suitable breeding habitat in Essex. It is likely that most of our winter rock pipits come across from the Baltic regions and are a subspecies distinct from the British breeding race. They specialise in feeding at the edges of the creeks and along the strandline.

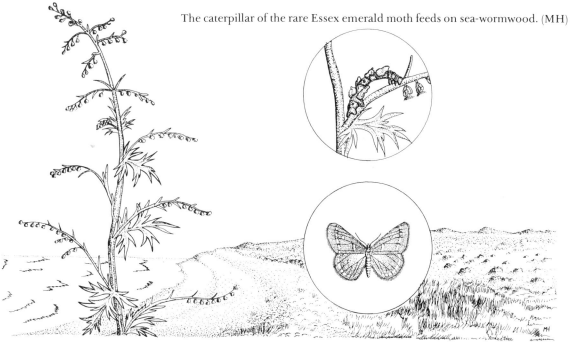

The caterpillar of the rare Essex emerald moth feeds on sea-wormwood. (MH)

The huge flocks of wildfowl and waders that are described in the section on estuaries move onto the saltmarshes as the incoming tide forces them off their mudflats. Most species feed little while on the saltmarsh, simply using it as a safe haven. An exception is the shelduck, which will bring its brood of ducklings, born in a nest burrow inside the seawall, to feed for their first few days of life, hidden amongst the saltmarsh plants.

In days before seawalls were built, many estuarine waders would also have fed on the shallow, almost freshwater lagoons which must have been a natural feature of the freshwater marsh between saltmarsh and woodland. These habitats have long gone but, at Fingringhoe, the ENT has created an entirely artificial habitat which mimics the lost lagoons. This is the 'scrape' on the upper part of the saltmarsh in Geedons Bay. When it was first built, the low seawall was frequently breached by the sea and the excavated lake became an artificial version of a saltpan. When, in 1981, the seawall was strengthened and a pump installed to bring fresh water from the large lake, it was possible to keep the scrape always at low salinity. This favours the rapid breeding of myriad invertebrates in the mud. Then the birds arrive to feed. It now regularly attracts large numbers of greenshank and spotted redshank, as well as many other species, to be watched and admired by the people in the nearby bird hides.

Saltmarshes are a dangerous place for birds to nest because of the constant threat of an extreme high tide flooding even the upper marsh. Redshanks are solitary breeders; about 1,100 pairs breed, scattered along the Essex coastal zones and many of these will nest, hidden in the upper marsh. Black-headed gulls are the other main salt-marsh nesters. They live in colonies, the main ones being on Rat Island in the Colne estuary and in part of Hamford Water. Over 5,000 pairs nest at these two sites. This compares with a total Essex breeding population of about 1,500 in 1938. The gulls have benefitted from all the food dumped on the coastal rubbish tips in recent decades.

Like nesting birds, caterpillars risk flooding and are restricted to the upper zone of the saltmarsh. Two British moths are virtually confined to the saltmarshes of Essex: the Essex emerald and the ground lackey. Both these species seem to have responded to the difficulty of living in England, at the very edge of their geographical ranges, by specialising in the saltmarsh habitat. On the continent of Europe these moths can be found in quite a wide range of habitats.

The Essex emerald was discovered in England in 1826 near Southend. It was later found along many of the saltmarshes on both sides of the Thames estuary. In recent years it has declined dramatically, probably because improvements to the seawalls have destroyed parts of the upper marsh where its foodplant (sea wormwood) grows. Herbicide drift and overgrazing may also have affected it. In the past, collecting by naturalists may also have reduced its range, but now the species is totally protected under the Wildlife and the Countryside Act, one of only five species of moth so protected. Today the Essex emerald survives in just one Essex and one Kent marsh. Fortunately part of the Essex locality is a nature reserve protected by the ENT.

Essex emerald caterpillars camouflage themselves successfully by attaching pieces of their foodplant to their body. The ground lackeys, in contrast, are protected by their fur and make a virtue of their conspicuousness. They live in colonies in silk tents over the plants on which they feed. This silk tent also provides an airfilled diving bell in which the caterpillars can survive a short submersion at high tide. Unlike their widespread close relative, the lackey, which feeds on trees, ground lackies feed on a variety of saltmarsh plants and are restricted to the Suffolk, Kent and Essex coasts. They are still common on many Essex saltmarshes, but there is some evidence that they are less widespread than formerly.

Saltmarshes are subject to many threats from man. Long ago, large areas of the upper marsh were cut off by the building of seawalls to claim land for agriculture. Marshland has been regarded as 'waste' which can be used for the most unsightly and dangerous purposes. Much of the Thames estuary marsh has gone, due to the construction of oil terminals and chemical works. Other areas, like Pitsea Marsh, have been used as infill sites to dump the contents of London's dustbins and rid the nation of chemicals too dangerous to dump elsewhere. The unspoilt marshes in the more attractive areas like Hamford Water (Arthur Ransome's setting for *Secret Water*) are demanded by developers for the building of marinas. Fortunately, the Trust has been successful, so far, in resisting the case for marinas in the most sensitive areas, but the planning applications and public enquiries continue unabated.

The high tides which bring in the silt that builds the saltmarshes nowadays bring in much plastic litter and leave it along the strandline. Much of this is thrown from ships into the North Sea, and waste from many countries can be spotted on the Essex marshes.

It is estimated that there are between 4,500 and 5,000 hectares of saltmarsh remaining in Essex; this is over 10% of the total for Britain. Most of this is within the large areas of coast designated as SSSIs of international or national importance. Within the last few years major parts of these SSSIs have been further protected by the areas outside the seawalls being included in major new national nature reserves (at Leigh, Dengie, Blackwater Estuary, Colne Estuary and Hamford Water). Eleven of the ENT reserves protect saltmarsh areas and two other saltmarshes are in RSPB and wildfowling reserves.

Several of these protected areas include examples of the other important Essex shoreline habitat: shell and shingle spits. These spits cover a total of 360 hectares — a tiny area compared with the saltmarshes. However, they are of major importance as nesting sites for seabirds as well as for their plant life.

Shingle beaches, where the wave action constantly shifts the shingle, are rather sterile habitats from a naturalist's point of view. Perhaps this is just as well, as most of them have been developed into seaside resorts anyway. The whole of the 20 kilometre stretch of sand and shingle beach from The Naze to St Osyth has suffered just this fate.

It is when shingle is drawn out by the currents and deposited into a spit, the upper parts of which are stable enough for some vegetation to develop, that shingle becomes an important wildlife habitat. The best example in Essex is the shingle spit at Colne Point, an ENT reserve.

'Stable enough for vegetation' does not mean that the shingle spit is a fixed feature. The corner of the Colne Point spit moved over 100m inland during an eight year period in the 1970s. Shrubby seablight is the nearest thing to a bush that grows on the shingle, and plays an important part in stabilising the higher parts of the shingle ridge. Yellow-horned poppies are beautiful plants, each flower lasting only a day before it withers to leave the pointed seed pod — its 'horn'. Sea campion is another attractive shore plant, only really plentiful at Colne Point.

Nearer the drift line, the earlier foreshore colonisers are saltwort, sea rocket, sea beet and several species of orache of which the commonest is hastate-leaved orache.

As well as its shingle spit, Colne Point is also important as one of the very few places in Essex where true sand dunes developed. Here marram grass holds the sand together and provides a root hold for sea spurge, sea bindweed and sea holly.

Apart from Colne Point, there are other important sand and shingle spits at the mouth of Hamford Water (Crabknowe Spit and Stone Point) within the area of the Hamford Water national nature reserve. To the south are several other spits, notably the ENT reserve at Bradwell and Foulness Point, where the spits are formed not from shingle but from shells. The 20 hectare shell beach in the Foulness SSSI is almost pure cockle shell and is the largest shell spit in Britain. The living cockles are buried in the mudflats. The tidal currents collect the dead shells and cast them up as a spit. The plants that colonise shell spits are much the same as those on shingle spits.

Perhaps the main interest of the shell and shingle spits is that they are major British breeding sites of the little tern and ringed plover. The 300 pairs of Essex ringed plovers are about 5% of the British total. Little terns have doubled their numbers in Essex between 1975 (204 pairs) and 1981 (421 pairs) and now represent 20% of the British breeding population.

Foulness Point is of major importance to both these species, and to the common terns — over half the Essex breeding pairs nest there. Ironically, the Maplin Airport Authority, which constituted the major threat to the most important wildlife habitats of Essex, created an artificial shell bank on Maplin Sands off Shoeburyness, before the plans for an airport were scrapped. This artificial spit has become one of the most important tern nesting sites!

Little tern with chick. (RH)

25

ABOVE: The demand for marinas is a constant development threat to saltmarshes. (DC) BELOW: Saltpans on the middle marsh at Colne Point. (SL)

ABOVE: Sea-lavender flowering on the Geedons saltmarsh. (DH) CENTRE: Saltpans frequently dry out completely until filled again by a high tide. (DH) BELOW: An eroded part of lower saltmarsh at Bradwell. (RG)

LEFT: A saltmarsh cliff where a creek cuts into the marsh. (SL) RIGHT: At high tide, saltmarsh creeks fill with water. (SL) BELOW: Shellbank breeding site of oystercatchers and ringed plovers. (RG)

LEFT: A bird observation tower and the ancient St Peter's church on the edge of the saltmarsh at Bradwell. (TI) RIGHT: Erosion is part of the natural process at Colne Point shingle beach. (DC) BELOW: Glasswort and annual seablight on a Bradwell saltmarsh. (RG)

ABOVE: A curlew, a grey plover and a flock of dunlin roost on a saltmarsh while high tide covers their feeding ground. (RG) BELOW: The courtship and ABOVE LEFT: mating of a pair of ringed plovers on a cockle shell beach. (RG)

30

RIGHT: A little tern broods two eggs in its beach nest at Colne Point; the Trust protects against foxes and holidaymakers. BELOW: Common cord-grass: a pioneer plant at the edge of a Colne estuary saltmarsh. (SL)

31

ABOVE: Shore-crabs live on the lower saltmarsh and in saltpan pools. (DC) BELOW: Sea-holly grows on the shingle spit at Colne Point. (MG) OPPOSITE: An infrared photograph taken by LANDSAT satellite showing Essex and surrounding areas. Woodlands reflect infrared strongly and show as dark red: Epping and Hatfield Forests show clearly. Reservoirs and deep sea show as dark blue. Mudflats and sandbanks are light blue as are urban areas. Not all red areas are woodland: permanent grassland also appears red. (RAE)

PLATE I

ABOVE: Aerial view of the shingle spit and salt-marsh at Colne Point nature reserve. (DC) CENTRE LEFT: Yellow-horned poppy in flower at Colne Point. (DH) RIGHT: A pair of common terns on their cockle-spit breeding site. (DH) BELOW: Shelduck courting and feeding. (RG)

PLATE II

Some common plants of the saltmarsh: LEFT: glasswort. (DC) ABOVE: sea-lavender; CENTRE: shrubby sea-blight; BELOW: sea purslane. (DH)

Leigh Marsh national nature reserve: with extensive eel-grass beds on the
mudflats. Saltmarsh fringes the seawall of Two Tree Island. (UCCFAP)

Mudflats and Estuaries

Common seals on Buxey Sand. (JF)

The most extensive and important wildlife habitats in Essex spend half the time under the sea. There are just over 20,000 hectares of mudflats and sandbanks within the boundaries of the major sites of special scientific interest on the Essex coast, from the Leigh marshes in the south to Hamford Water and the Stour estuary in the north.

The majority of these huge flats are so important as the main feeding grounds for vast flocks of estuarine birds, that the Nature Conservancy Council has designated them in the top priority category (1*): sites of international importance. All of the designated flats are at least grade 1, equivalent in importance to national nature reserves, and recently the designation of several coastal national nature reserves has given parts of the flats some extra protection.

The only major areas of Essex mudflat not designated as SSSIs are the Mucking Flats and the 'beach' at Southend-on-Sea, crossed by the longest pier in Britain. Offshore are some island flats: Buxey Sand off the Dengie peninsula and Gunfleet Sand off Clacton cover 3,000 hectares at low tide. They have no special protection but are nonetheless important wildlife habitats. The only known breeding site of the common seal in Essex is on the Buxey Sand.

'Common seal' is rather a misnomer: in Britain there are many more grey seals, breeding on rocky shores and islets, than there are common seals. No grey seals breed on Essex shores, although a few non-breeders have been seen fishing the Essex seas. Female common seals haul themselves up on to Buxey Sand in late June or early July to give birth. The pup can swim with its mother within an hour or two of birth, which is just as well since, by then, the tide will be flooding back across the temporarily exposed sandbank.

The range between high and low water is about 4½ metres: a vertical range that is enough to uncover up to five or six kilometres of mudflat between the lower edge of the saltmarsh and low tide mark. Offshore, the faster currents allow only sands to be deposited: hence the Buxey and Gunfleet Sands. Inshore, the sheltered conditions allow the build up of mudflats from extremely fine clay particles washed down the estuaries and off the saltmarshes.

The soft mud and extremely rapid flooding by the incoming tide make mudflats dangerous places for humans to explore. The danger is compounded because much of the area lies within the target zone of coastal firing ranges. It is still possible to explore the flats on a trackway that has been used by man since prehistoric times. The 'Broomway' is a public right of way which runs from Wakering Stairs to Fisherman's Head on Foulness Island.

The name 'Foulness' may well conjure up a picture of an extremely unpleasant area. This prejudice will be reinforced when, treading in soft mud, the foul vapours are released from the region below the surface where bacteria, in the absence of oxygen, are doing their job of breaking down the organic content of the mud. But 'Foul'ness does not refer to the stink of disturbed mud; it is an altered spelling of 'Fowl'ness: the home of myriad waders and waterfowl.

If any one species of wildfowl is responsible for the name 'Fowlness' it must be the brent goose. More brent geese feed on the Maplin and Foulness flats than at any other place in the world. In recent years, when the world population of these geese has been at a record high, there have been up to 20,000 geese on these flats at once.

Apart from a few light-bellied brent geese in most winters, the Essex brent geese are the dark-bellied race. They breed in the Siberian tundra and winter on the tidal flats bordering the North Sea. Until the population explosion of the last twenty years, Essex was the winter haunt of half the dark-bellied brent geese in the world. Now, although the present Essex total is equal to the world total of twenty years ago, the increased Essex population is only half the British total and about one seventh the world total.

Three factors have combined to increase the goose population. Eel grass, the main food of the geese when they are feeding on the mudflats, suffered a major disease in the 1930s. Now the eel grass is recovering, and geese have also learnt to exploit extra grazing inside the seawall. At a time when the goose population was low, international pressure encouraged all the countries in which the geese winter to ban the shooting of brent geese. The main factor that limits the goose population is the success, or otherwise, of each breeding season in the extreme and variable conditions of Siberia. A succession of good breeding seasons, combined with winter protection from shooting and an adequate food resource, allowed the population to increase five-fold between 1972 and 1981. Now a poor breeding season may have halted or reversed the trend.

The threat to the Maplin Sands, posed by the possible development of the third London airport at Maplin, was the stimulus for a most detailed study of the ecology of this region, carried out by the Natural Environment Research Council in the mid-1970s. One of the main discoveries concerned the feeding behaviour of brent geese. It had long been known that the geese feed on eel grass. But ordinary eel grass loses its leaves in autumn before the brent geese arrive. It is the slightly rarer species, dwarf eel-grass, that is so important. The returning brent geese fly first to the main areas of dwarf eel-grass on the Leigh and Maplin flats. When they have exhausted this food supply, they switch to other food or disperse to other feeding areas.

The annual growth of dwarf eel-grass has been carefully estimated. Most of it grows on the Foulness and Maplin flats where the 325 hectare bed is the largest continuous population of dwarf eel-grass in Europe. This bed alone produced an estimated 184 tonnes of leaves in 1973. The brent geese eat nearly all of it. In some areas they spend so much time feeding, that they have to dig up the eel-grass roots because they have eaten all the leaves. So, as the goose population has increased, it has considerably overgrazed its main natural food.

There is another food plant on the flats: the alga *Enteromorpha*. When supported by the incoming tide, this alga looks like masses of green guts: hence the scientific name *Enteromorpha intestinalis*. There is a much larger area of mudflat with *Enteromopha* than with dwarf eel-grass and each hectare produces two tonnes of alga compared with a little over half a tonne per hectare for dwarf eel-grass. But the alga has a much higher water content and geese would have to eat four times the weight of alga to get the same nourishment that they get from dwarf eel-grass. They do eat the alga, but only when they have run out of eel-grass.

The eel-grasses are a rare example of a rooted plant, evolved from land-based ancestors, that have adapted to a marine life. Apart from *Enteromorpha* and smaller amounts of the sea-lettuce, *Ulva,* large algae are rare on mudflats, although where a large stone provides an attachment point, clumps of bladder wrack and knotted wrack can be found. The important plants of most mudflats are microscopic: tiny diatoms and blue-green algae exist as a thin slime over the whole surface of the flats and provide one of the main food resources for the abundant animal life of the mud.

Feeding on the surface of the mud are huge numbers of small snails. The size of grape pips, these *Hydrobia* snails can exist at densities of up to 16,000 to a square metre. In the surface layers of the mud are mudhopper crustaceans called *Corophium*. These two tiny organisms make up the bulk of the food of the smaller waders. The smallest and commonest wader, the dunlin, takes mostly *Hydrobia*. So do knot, although they prefer a small bivalve mollusc, *Macoma,* which is also common near the surface of the mud. Redshank specialise in *Corophium.*

The invertebrates which live on or near the surface of the mud get moved around by the incoming tide — which is why the strandline of the advancing tide is such a good feeding site for the smaller waders.

Deeper in the mud are ragworms, *Nereis* and *Nephthys,* favoured food of the curlew, which also takes larger specimens of *Macoma.*

Although mud and sandflats harbour huge numbers of invertebrates, any one area has a small number of different species. Five or ten species living in a small area of mud is about the norm. But the flats vary a great deal in ways important to the invertebrate animals. The most sheltered areas have soft mud with an anaerobic layer just below the surface. Other flats consist of sandy particles mixed with mud; they are firmer and oxygen penetrates deeper into the sand. Where currents flow faster, the sand is topped with stones and shells. This variation in the structure of the flats, together with the variation in the time the flat is exposed to the air at low-tide, means that, even though one small area supports only a few species of invertebrate, the whole flat may harbour fifty or a hundred different species.

Some of the most detailed studies of the marine animal life in Essex estuaries and flats were carried out by scientists employed by the Central Electricity Generating Board, to investigate the Blackwater estuary, where the Bradwell nuclear power station discharges warmed water into the sea. It seems that the area warmed by the waste waters has about the same diversity of animal life as parts of the estuary remote from the power station. Perhaps this is not surprising, as estuarine animals have to be more tolerant of temperature changes than fully marine ones. Shallow waters flooding in across hot summer sands can reach high temperatures and in hard winters the estuary may freeze.

The sandflats (or flats of sand and mud mixed) have larger invertebrates which can burrow deeper because oxygen is available. The most important species are the lugworm, favoured food of the bar-tailed godwits, and the cockles in which the oystercatcher specialises.

Osytercatchers can open oysters if they get the chance, but oysters are rarely exposed even at the lowest of tides. Cockles and mussels are their main food. Mussels are common wherever there is something solid for them to grow on. The larval stage in the plankton attaches to a fixed stone, mooring post, or areas of stable shingle, and grows to the fixed adult mussel only if its mooring is not washed away. Cockles, buried in the sand, are much more widespread. They have been found at densities of up to 400 per square metre on the north shore of the Blackwater.

An oystercatcher feeding on cockles by day will spot the telltale signs on the surface that reveal where the cockle is buried. It then probes with its beak and, with sideways movements of its head, levers the cockle out of the mud. Then the oystercatcher opens its catch by bashing it with its powerful beak. Oystercatchers, like most waders, also feed at night. Then they have to rely on a sense of touch to find the cockles. They walk along making sewing movements, moving their beaks from side to side through the mud, until a cockle is touched.

Waders can only feed when the mudflats are exposed by the tide: at high tide they roost, usually in the adjacent saltmarshes. They need to make good use of the feeding time when the tide is out: for example, dunlin spend three-quarters of each tide cycle feeding. Waders can find huge amounts of food: typically an oystercatcher eats 40% of its own body weight each day.

It is the rare vagrant waders, like black-winged stilts (ten records in Essex since the war), that attract a mass migration of bird-watchers to the hides at the coastal nature reserves. But it is the huge numbers of the common species that make the Essex flats of international conservation importance, as well as providing one of the most impressive wildlife spectacles in Essex. Detailed surveys in the mid-1970s provided the best available figures for the numbers of waders in Essex. The average mid-winter population is 123,000.

Most of these waders do not stay in Essex to breed. Knot, grey plovers and sanderling breed in the arctic tundras. Dunlin and curlew move to the moorlands of northern Britain. Black-tailed godwits may also breed on low-lying ground inland. But none of these species is known to breed in Essex, although non-breeding individuals are always to be seen summering on the Essex coast.

Oystercatchers, redshank and ringed plovers all breed in Essex although, in each case, the winter population is much higher than the summer breeding population. The estuarine waders include quite large numbers of lapwing and golden plovers, but the majority of the wintering population of these two species feeds on ploughed fields inland.

The following figures give a clear idea of the international importance of the Essex flats for wintering waders. The table includes only those species where more than one percent of the European population winters in Essex (one percent is the usual definition of a population of international importance). For each species, the normal Essex winter population (to the nearest 100) is given, and the percentage of the total European population that this represents.

Species			Species			Species	mid-1970s	% Europe	1982
Dunlin	69,000	5½%	Ringed plover	1,000	5½%				
Redshank	12,000	9½%	Turnstone	1,100	?	Brent goose	15,500	19½%	22,200
Knot	11,000	2%	Bar-tailed godwit	2,100	5½%	Shelduck	7,700	6%	11,200
Curlew	7,000	4½%	Black-tailed godwit	600	1½%	Wigeon	6,100	2%	17,500
Oystercatcher	7,000	1%	Sanderling	400	4%	Teal	2,400	1½%	7,000
Grey plover	2,500	8½%				Pintail	900	1½%	2,100

Not only is the total Essex population of these species of international importance, the flocks of waders in the individual estuaries are too. Not all the estuaries are equally attractive to all species: for example, the main concentration of bar-tailed godwits is at Foulness, while most black-tailed godwits are in the Stour estuary and Hamford Water. The sanderling are most common on the sand beaches fronting the Walton/Frinton/Clacton conurbation. With the exception of the Crouch and Roach estuaries and the Thames upriver of Leigh, all Essex estuaries and major flats contain internationally important populations of at least three wader species.

In addition to all the waders that spend the winter on the Essex flats, there are others which are purely passage migrants. In spring they move northwards to their breeding grounds and return southwards in autumn. Little stints and curlew sandpipers are good examples of regular, but rather scarce, passage migrants. Greenshank and common sandpipers are more abundant.

At the spring and autumn passage, not only are there all the extra species present, but the numbers of the winter visitors are boosted by additional birds on passage. Fortunately the passage occurs at the two times of year when feeding on the flats is easiest: in autumn the invertebrates are at peak abundance, in spring they are less common but the ones that are there are at their largest size and make good eating for the birds.

In addition to the brent geese, Essex estuaries harbour many other types of wildfowl. Thirteen species of duck are seen regularly and four of these, all surface feeders, have internationally important Essex populations. Like the wader information, these statistics were gathered in the mid-1970s and wildfowl populations have been increasing in the county since then. The table also gives details of the January 1982 figures (the most recent mid-winter figures available) for comparison, but January 1982 was a time of abnormally high wildfowl populations on the Essex coast.

Although not always as spectacular and exciting as the wildfowl and waders, the estuaries contain several hundred species of marine animals and many of these will begin feeding on the mudflats as the tide rises and the birds are forced off to their roosts.

The Electricity Board's survey of the Blackwater/Colne estuary gives a fascinating insight into the diversity of marine life in a typical Essex estuary. At the top end of the size scale were three mammals. Porpoises and common seals fish in the estuary and, in 1962, a fin whale was stranded at Brightlingsea.

Twenty-two species of fish were recorded as common in the estuary. Flatfish are especially well adapted to life in shallow waters with a muddy or sandy bottom. Dab, plaice, sole and flounders are common, commercially important species. Of the fish that swim actively in open water, rather than resting and feeding on the bottom, whiting and small cod are common and sprats are so abundant as to form a major local fishery. Because of the warm waters and rich feeding, estuaries are important breeding grounds for many fish that will complete their growth further out to sea. The Blackwater is a major spawning site for herring.

Inshore fishing is still a fairly important local industry on the Essex coast, and the Government maintains a fisheries research laboratory at Burnham-on-Crouch. Here the range of fish species is similar to the Blackwater estuary. It is usually possible for interested naturalists to charter a small trawler at Burnham and be given a chance to see the marine life only normally familiar to the fishermen. Arrangements have to be made well in advance. The trawl will bring up huge numbers of spider crabs, starfish, sunstars and brittle-stars as well as a variety of edible fish.

Ninety-six species of mollusc have been found in the Blackwater estuary. The common species of the tidal flats, so important to the waders, have already been mentioned; the species of most interest to man is a sublittoral one — the oyster. Between low water-mark and a depth of six metres oysters occur wherever a firm mud bottom is covered with fragments of shell. The shell fragments

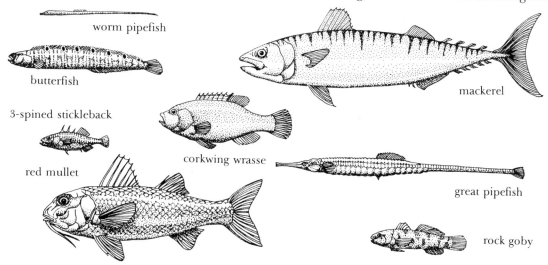

worm pipefish

butterfish

mackerel

3-spined stickleback

corkwing wrasse

red mullet

great pipefish

rock goby

These are a few of over 80 species of marine and estuarine fish that have
returned to the tidal Thames since pollution levels were reduced. (CA)

and stones to which the larval oysters (spat) attach is called cultch and is often added to by oyster-fishermen to increase the size of the oyster beds.

Essex oysters have been world-famous since Roman times. At Fingringhoe Wick nature reserve, gravel workings have cut through Roman kitchen middens, and the layers of oyster shells attest to the enthusiasm with which oysters were eaten by the residents of the Roman villas at Fingringhoe. The characteristic flat shells of native English oysters have been found in archaeological excavations at Rome itself — so clearly the export trade developed early. 'Poor Britons — there is some good in them after all — they produce an oyster' wrote the Roman, Sallust, in 50 BC.

Some of the earliest conservation laws applied in Essex were for the protection of oysters. In 1577, dredging the Thames for oysters was forbidden between Easter and Lammastide: that is, during the oysters' spawning season. The first charter of Colchester, Britain's oldest chartered town, recorded, in 1189, the rights to the oysters of the Colne estuary enjoyed by the townsfolk 'from time immemorial'.

At one time Colchester 'green' oysters were especially prized. The gills of oysters go green when they have been feeding on the huge numbers of diatoms which develop in warm shallow water, where evaporation has raised the natural salinity. In many Essex creeks, reached only by the highest tides, these conditions would occur naturally; but oysters were also transferred to saltmarsh pools to encourage greening.

In Victorian times, oysters from the Essex estuaries were dredged in huge numbers and shipped to London. In one year (1864) 496 million oysters passed through the Billingsgate market: perhaps not all of them came from Essex! At that time oysters were appreciated mainly by the poor: 'poverty and oysters seem always to go together' says Dickens' Sam Weller.

The elements of oyster farming have been known since Roman times. As well as laying cultch to encourage natural spat fall, young oysters can be dredged and then replaced, spaced out on private oyster grounds to fatten. Natural spat falls are unpredictable, the Colne estuary being one of the few areas where native oysters reproduce successfully. Increasingly the oyster fishermen relied on imported young oysters to be fattened in Essex estuaries.

At the end of the 19th century, American oysters were imported to Essex. They did not do well and are now extinct, but the oyster pests they brought with them have thrived exceedingly. The American slipper limpet lives in the same habitat as oysters and, through its abundance and its excrement changing the nature of the mud, can be a serious competitor with oysters. Densities of up to 2,000 per square metre have been recorded in Blackwater. The American oyster drill is a kind of whelk and a direct predator of young oysters. It, too, has become common in Essex estuaries.

Today great efforts are being made to restore the Essex oyster fisheries, although there are considerable problems caused by an outbreak of oyster disease and by the toxic effects of the anti-fouling paints applied to the bottoms of all the leisure boats. Native oysters are the main species but Portuguese oysters are also imported for fattening. These have the advantage that they grow well in the cool Essex waters but do not waste energy spawning. But, in complete contrast to Victorian times, the pleasure of swallowing a mouthful of sea-water contained in the living flesh of a mutilated mollusc is reserved for the rich.

Eighty-eight species of crustaceans have been recorded in the Blackwater estuary. Most of these are tiny members of the plankton. Several species of barnacle can be found attached to submerged stones or the shells of oysters, continually filtering the water with their feathered legs to collect their food particles. The commonest species in estuaries is *Elminius*: a native of New Zealand, it was introduced to British waters by shipping at the end of the second world war.

Shore crabs are common on the flats and saltmarshes, moving to a fully submerged habitat as they grow larger. Large lobsters are rather rare, limited by the lack of suitable hiding places. They can be found living in the protection of submerged wrecks and are common enough to make it worthwhile for Thames estuary fishermen to lay lobster pots.

Two species of shrimp are the basis of another fishing industry. The common (brown) shrimp is common on both clean and muddy bottoms in the mouths of estuaries. The pink shrimp feeds on a tube living marine worm *(Sabellaria)* and the rubble of the worms' characteristic tubes (called 'ross') is a good guide to where the shrimps will be found. Including *Sabellaria*, 67 species of marine polychaete worms are known in the Blackwater estuary.

In summer, common jellyfish and the strangely beautiful sea-gooseberries drift up the estuaries. They are just the largest and most obvious members of an abundant plankton. The peak summer plankton consists of a mix of the larval stages of the many sedentary animals, plus the myriad small 'full-time' members of the plankton, most of which are copepod crustaceans. In summer, a litre of estuary water contains about 100 planktonic animals.

The Thames estuary is rather different from the smaller Essex estuaries, not simply due to its size, but because, until recently, it was one of the most grossly polluted rivers in Britain. The invention of the water closet in the 19th century allowed the burgeoning city population to discharge its sewage, untreated, into the centre of London, and the river became a stinking sewer, completely uninhabited by fish, downstream from London.

Seven thousand human deaths a year from cholera in the epidemics of the 1840s failed to convince the Government that something should be done. But by 1856 the Thames was so foul that the stink made the Houses of Parliament unbearable. Then action was swift, and a new sewer took most of London's sewage to be discharged, still raw, at Becton in Essex. The northern outfall sewer is the largest tributary of the Thames and all that untreated sewage meant the Essex reach of the Thames remained a dead river.

The late 1950s saw the first real effort to clean the Thames. New works treated all the sewage before discharge. The treated sewage had already been decayed by bacteria and so it did not deplete the dissolved oxygen in the river. As oxygen returned, so did the fish. From the late 1960s, increasing numbers and species of sea fish have been found in the Thames. At the most recent count, over 80 species had been recorded. This is an almost incredible success story of which the Thames Water Authority is justly proud.

The mouth of the Thames supports inshore shrimping and fishing industries and one very strange industry: the collection of 'white weed'. White weed is actually a colonial animal — a hydroid colony that grows attached to the river bottom and releases miniature jellyfish *(medusae)* into the plankton. The white weed is dredged up and dyed bright green for use as decoration in aquaria. At least this used to be the case, but in recent years aquarists have preferred to use artificial pond weeds of mineral (plastic) origin rather than dyed dead animals. The white weed is still abundant but the industry is in decline.

Another Thames industry, also declining and also associated with pet fish keeping, is *Tubifex* collecting. *Tubifex* are bright red worms that live in the mud of estuaries where sea-water is diluted by river water. They are tolerant of pollution because their red haemoglobin enables them to store oxygen, and so survive periods of extremely low dissolved oxygen. The mud of the inner Thames estuary used to be coloured red by dense *Tubifex* populations, which were collected and sold as live food for aquarium fish.

Brent goose feeding on eel-grass. (RH)

ABOVE LEFT: Laurie Forsyth, warden of the Fingringhoe Wick nature reserve, investigates the layers of oysters and broken pottery dating from Roman times. (TI) RIGHT: A redshank on a Dengie mudflat. (RG) BELOW LEFT: A grey plover quickly pulls a ragworm from its burrow. (RG) RIGHT: The tracks of brent geese on a mudflat. (DH)

ABOVE: Bar-tailed godwits at Bradwell. (RG) CENTRE: A curlew sleeps while bar-tailed godwits preen. (RG) BELOW: Dunlin roost. (RG)

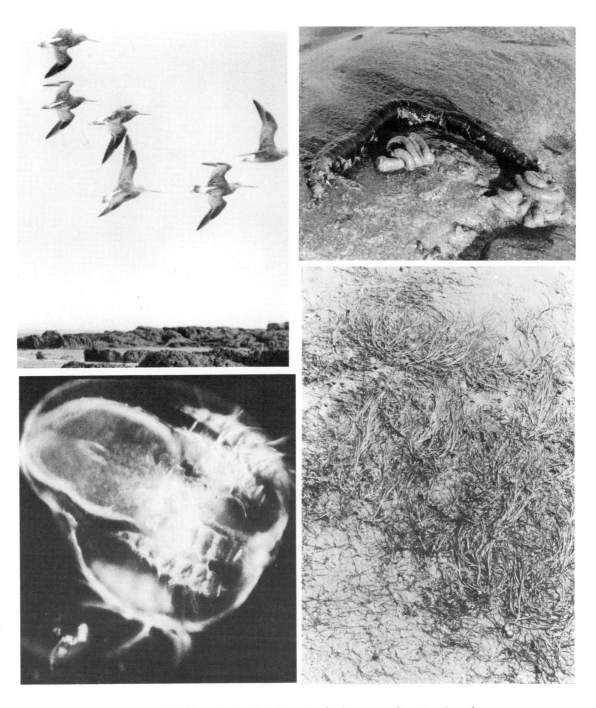

ABOVE LEFT: Bar-tailed godwits leave the feeding grounds at Dengie as the tide rises. (RG) RIGHT: Lugworms are a favourite food of curlew and bar-tailed godwit. (RG) BELOW LEFT: A transparent sea-gooseberry from the plankton of an Essex estuary. (DC) RIGHT: Eel-grass and dwarf-grass on an Essex mudflat. (DH)

ABOVE: Dunlin landing at Bradwell. (RG) LEFT: A sea-slater ventures out
at night on to the barnacle-covered supports of the Fingringhoe Wick jetty.
(DC) RIGHT: *Hydrobia* snails crawl over cockle shells on an Essex shore-line.
(DH)

ABOVE: The red crag cliffs at the Naze; frequent landslips reveal new fossils. (UCCFAP) BELOW: Skippers Island nature reserve in Hamford Water. Note the breached seawall and partially wooded areas protected by the inner walls. Horsey Island is in the background. (UCCFAP)

Seawalls and Islands

Brown hare on a coastal grazing marsh. (JF)

If you were to sail a boat from London down the Thames and then up the Essex coast to Harwich, the journey would cover about 140 kilometres. But on the journey you would have passed the mouths of numerous creeks and estuaries, which repeatedly lead the sea deep inland. It is the protection of this heavily indented coastline that has necessitated building over 500 kilometres of seawall.

Two pressures have led to the investment of so much time and money in building seawalls. Essex has been sinking at the rate of about 25 cm a century since Roman times. It is said that at certain tides a Roman could cross the Blackwater (on horseback) from the Othona fort on the south shore to Mersea on the north. As the centuries passed, previously dry inhabited land has increasingly been at risk of flooding. Also, by walling the sea out of the upper saltmarsh, much more valuable pasture (and, in recent years, arable land) can be claimed for farming. Seawalls, then, are a product of need and greed. Never has the need been more forcefully demonstrated than on the last night of January 1953. The highest tide ever recorded, whipped up by easterly gales, breached the seawalls along much of the Essex coast. 119 people died, 12,356 homes were flooded and the sea covered 16,700 hectares of farmland.

The Great Tide led to a massive programme of seawall improvements and other defences, of which the Thames barrage is the latest to become operational. Amongst the immediate effects of the flood was the temporary return of salt-marsh plants to arable land. The following summer two Essex botanists, on a visit to Foulness Island, were amazed to find giant specimens of branched glasswort and annual seablight that had grown to over a metre high in the fertile conditions of a sea-flooded ploughed field.

The defences built along the coast during the Roman period were more concerned with defending Essex against invading Saxons than against invading sea. It was in Norman times that seawall building began in earnest. By 1210 the 'law of the marsh' forced everyone who owned, or had rights on marshland to contribute towards the cost of sea defences. This system continued until 1930, when the Land Drainage Act created Government agencies to do the work.

In a few places the land rises out of the saltmarsh steeply enough to make an artificial seawall unnecessary. In sheltered estuaries, the forces of erosion do not create a cliff, and a natural transition from marsh to woodland, via grassland, occurs. The best example of this is where the scrub-covered Ray Island (a National Trust property managed by the ENT) rises out of Bonner's Saltings between Mersea Island and the mainland. Bonner's Saltings, too, are a nature reserve. At low tide it is possible to walk across the saltings to the island and then be trapped on a real island at high tide.

In slightly less sheltered conditions, where woodland remains adjacent to a saltmarsh, a small mud cliff marks high-water mark and provides a sudden transition from marsh to wood. The most important such area is Copperas Bay on the Stour estuary. The RSPB owns 74 hectares of saltings and mudflats. Adjacent to the bay are two ancient woodlands: Stour Wood owned by the Woodland Trust and Copperas Wood, which runs right to the shoreline, owned by the Essex Naturalists' Trust. It is here, at the natural junction of marsh and wood, that the rare marsh mallow plant survives. 'Copperas' is a bisulphide of iron that, until the 1870s, was mined in the area to make green vitriol for dyeing and for use as an ink.

The only true cliffs in Essex are at the Naze at Walton. These cliffs are a classic site for geological studies and it is mainly for this reason that they have been designated a site of special scientific interest. The red crag deposits which form the cliffs are one of the more recent geological deposits in Essex, having been formed just before the onset of the ice ages. The sandy nature of the red crag, the mix of land and sea fossils and the fact that the deposits are steeply cross bedded, show that the red crag formed as a shore line or offshore sand bank.

One of the most common and characteristic fossils of the Naze cliffs is a whelk *(Neptunia contraria)* whose shell is coiled anticlockwise. In other respects the 'left-handed' whelk was similar to present day species. Mammal remains include the bones of mammoths, giant deer and rhinoceros that would have roamed Essex in pre-ice age times.

The Naze cliffs are subject to frequent land-slips and erosion. Defences against the sea have been constructed at the foot of the cliffs, but the real problem comes from water draining through the red crag sands and being trapped above the London clay deposits. This internal lubrication causes slumping and slipping. The process has been going on for a long time: Walton parish church disappeared over the cliff in 1798 and its former site is now well out to sea. Bungalows built some distance from the cliffs between the wars now have the cliff edge advancing up the garden path towards them.

The soft soil and frequent landslips make the cliffs unsuitable as nesting areas for cliff-nesting seabirds, although fulmars have been seen prospecting the area. But the cliffs are ideal for sand martins. The two regular breeding colonies on the Essex cliffs are the only examples of natural breeding sites in Essex. Almost all the other 46 known colonies are on inland 'cliffs' created by sand and gravel digging.

In the Essex estuaries, and rising gently out of the saltmarshes, are many islands. With rare exceptions, like Ray Island, these are protected by seawalls built to convert the islands to grazing marshes. It is difficult to know how many Essex islands there are. Does a tiny piece of raised salt-marsh on a mudflat count as an island? Many of the larger islands are connected to land by artificial causeways — are they still islands? Some of the smaller islands cease to be islands at low-tide. And the final problem is that some inter-island tidal creeks have been dammed and converted to freshwater dykes. In this way, Havengore and New England islands have been joined to Foulness island. But, just counting those islands big enough to be mapped as islands on the Ordnance Survey 1:250,000 (quarter inch to the mile) Atlas of Great Britain, there are over 30 Essex islands — a total equal to the whole of the rest of the eastern half of England.

The three biggest islands all have full-scale human communities on them and have good roads connecting them to the mainland. The smaller islands are mostly uninhabited or have a single farmhouse. The three big islands make an interesting contrast with one another. Mersea has a small seaside resort at the west end of the island: a fairly typical mix of holiday homes, boats and caravans and many retired residents. The rest of the island is agricultural land. The Mersea flats are an important part of the Colne Estuary National Nature Reserve and are adjoined by the only bit of woodland on the island: Cudmore Grove country park.

ABOVE: Redshank: feeding in a shallow pool, and display behaviour. (RG) BELOW LEFT: A lone curlew on a Dengie mudflat. (RG) RIGHT: A harvest mouse climbs among seed-heads; these mice are often found where saltmarsh grades into reed beds. (DC)

PLATE III

ABOVE: A bluebell carpet at Weeleyhall Wood. (DC) LEFT: Oxlips are a special feature of ancient woods on the chalky boulder clay. (DC) RIGHT: Primroses on the boundary bank of the Roman River Nature Reserve. (DC)

PLATE IV

Canvey Island is an intensely industrial and populated area. Half the island has been built up with cheap and nasty housing. The island also has a mass of oil terminals, storage tanks and chemical factories and there are many more next to the island at Coryton and Thames Haven. It is the ever-present danger of factory explosions or fires, rather than the risk of a repeat of the 1953 'Great Tide', that makes Canvey Island rank as one of the most dangerous places to live in Britain. Escape routes, colour coded, are signed at every road junction and evacuation plans practised frequently.

A much less extreme danger on Canvey Island, literally a minor irritation, is caused by the abundance of brown-tail moth caterpillars. These hairy caterpillars live in nests on hawthorn, blackthorn and other bushes. The nest is spun by the hundred or so caterpillars that hatch from a single batch of eggs and in their nest they spend the winter. In spring and summer the caterpillars grow quickly and are protected from birds by their covering of irritant hairs. Some people are sensitive to these hairs and develop a severe rash from contact with the caterpillars. Brown-tail moths, especially common on Canvey, are found around much of the Essex coast and seem to be spreading upriver and inland. Public complaints have led to insecticide spraying of hedgerows and roadside shrubs.

Curiously, another hairy caterpillar that lives in tents on rosaceous shrubs had its main Essex centre on Canvey island. This is the small eggar: once widespread in England, it has declined dramatically. There have been no certain records in Essex since 1970 and it may be extinct.

Foulness has a small human population: in recent times this is because the island is closed to public access by the Ministry of Defence. The number of inhabited houses, around 100, has hardly changed since the middle of the 19th century. Early records from the 16th to 19th centuries record Foulness as an unhealthy place to live: always damp, often flooded and no regular supply of fresh-water. Few people chose to live on the island and those who did were 'rough, lawless and offensive to decency'. Usually there were twice as many men as women. Modern censuses show a normal civilian population: an equal sex ratio and mainly law-abiding folk. But the undisclosed numbers of military men on the island must maintain the traditional imbalance between the sexes. Inside its sea-walls, Foulness has the most interesting grazing marshes in Essex with a rich diversity of flowering plants.

Some of the smaller islands were never walled in and converted to grazing marsh. Uninhabited and difficult of access, both by man and predatory mammals, they are good breeding areas for black-headed gulls. The colony on Rat Island, an ENT reserve in the Colne estuary, has increased to between 3,000 and 4,000 pairs in recent years. There is also a big colony on some of the saltmarsh islands in Hamford Water. All these colonies suffer from flooding at very high tides, and the Rat Island colony has recently been inundated annually. The gulls have begun to move to a nearby freshwater marsh where they may harm other wildlife. The once large gullery on Horsey Island has declined in recent years due to foxes.

On some walled islands the grazing ceased because of difficulties of access, and then the seawall may have been left unrepaired after a breach. Saltmarsh then develops inside the old seawall. This has happened on Bridgemarsh Island in the Crouch estuary — now an important wildfowl area owned by a wildfowling society. Skipper's Island in Hamford Water, now an ENT reserve, also has a breached seawall. The Trust is working to repair part of an inner wall, since the freshwater pools and grasslands maintain a more diverse and endangered range of wildlife than the saltmarsh on the island. Grazing on Skipper's Island ceased before the second war, and wartime attempts to restart ended in disaster when the cattle wandered off the causeway and sank in deep mud.

The late E.F. Williams purchased Skipper's Island in 1955. Between then and 1972, when he generously gave the Trust a 999 year lease on the land, he loved to stay on the island and study its wildlife. He encouraged many members of the Essex Field Club to visit and study the island and publish their findings in the *Essex Naturalist*.

E.F. Williams was the Essex recorder for butterflies and moths, so it must have been exciting when a species of moth new to Britain was found breeding in the area — but perhaps a little annoying that is was someone else who made the discovery! Fisher's estuarine moth was discovered in 1968 by J.B. Fisher. It is the only large moth whose sole British population is in Essex — and the reason for its restriction is that its caterpillar stage feeds only in the stem of Hog's fennel. This plant has been known from the Hamford Water area for several centuries: it is still quite common on the seawalls and islands and sometimes even grows on the roadside. But Hamford Water and a site near Faversham in Kent are the only places in Britain where Hog's fennel is found.

Fisher's estuarine moth has a life cycle similar to that of its close relative, the frosted orange. The difference is that frosted orange caterpillars feed inside the stems of thistles, so the species is widespread and common. Apparently, Fisher's estuarine moth has not colonised the Kent Hog's fennel and is restricted to Hamford Water. It is just as well that the ENT protects good populations of both foodplant and moth on Skipper's Island, as there have been many cases of unscrupulous moth collectors digging up the plants to find the moth pupae. Although the moth is a recent discovery it has almost certainly been established in the area for many years. The *Victoria County History,* published at the turn of the century, records a 'large, pale form of the frosted orange' from the Hamford Water area. This can only have been Fisher's estuarine moth.

The largest and most recent Essex island nature reserve is Northey Island, in the Blackwater estuary. The island was donated to the National Trust, with some farmland on the adjacent mainland, in 1978. Nearly 1,000 years before that, in 991, occurred the dramatic Battle of Maldon. Vikings landed on Northey Island and demanded tribute from the East Saxons. Because it would be unsporting to slaughter enemies as they crossed the narrow causeway from the island to the mainland, Bryhtnoth, the Essex leader, allowed the Vikings to cross unhindered and form their battle lines on what is now South House Farm. The noble gesture was misguided, the battle lost, Bryhtnoth killed, and the Vikings departed with a 'tribute' of 'x thusend punda'. One of the escaping Essex noblemen recorded the heroic defeat in 325 alliterative verses — one of the best of the surviving Old English poems.

Today the same narrow causeway, covered each high tide, is still the only access to Northey Island. And today a new form of 'tribute' is being paid to invading hordes from the north — brent geese. In recent years the increased population of geese has overgrazed its traditional eel grass beds and started to move inside the seawalls to graze on the succulent grass fields. Now that many of the grazing marshes have been ploughed up, the geese have started on the winter cereal fields. Farmers claim that the geese cause a great deal of damage — more by their feet compacting the ground than the actual amount eaten.

Once the geese have established a habit of feeding in an area it is difficult to scare them off — even when the farmers have been given licences to shoot limited numbers of geese. On Northey Island, and a few other coastal areas of Essex, a new ploy has proved effective. Certain grass fields, where the geese will do little harm, have been made attractive by fertilising the grass crop (using fertilisers donated by the manufacturers) and plastic model geese, in the feeding position, set up in the field. Seeing the models safely feeding, wild geese join them by the hundred. Nearby fields can be protected from the geese by placing model geese in the 'head-up' warning position and with plastic fertiliser sacks mounted on poles. Over two thousand geese were fed and protected on the special 'goose field' on Northey Island in the winter of 1982 — the first time the scheme was tried.

Building seawalls created grazing marsh out of saltmarsh. It is estimated that around 15,000 hectares of saltmarsh have been lost in this way in Essex. But the conversion to freshwater grazing marsh produced a rich new range of wildlife habitats, now being lost at a frightening rate as old marshlands are deep drained and ploughed to add to the growing European grain mountain.

A detailed habitat survey of Essex coastal grasslands, carried out in the 1970s by the Natural Environment Research Council, showed that the richness of these habitats was a result of the grassland being a complex of sub-habitats, each with its own variety of species. The survey was based mainly on the numbers of flowering plant species: the richest marshes, on Foulness, had over 200 species but the norm for a smaller study area was around 50 or 60. Apart from the closely grazed areas, with a limited number of species, eight sub-habitats contributed to the species richness.

The seawall itself counts as two sub-habitats, as the seaward side of the wall has a distinctly different mix of species compared to the more sheltered, and species rich, landward side. Slender

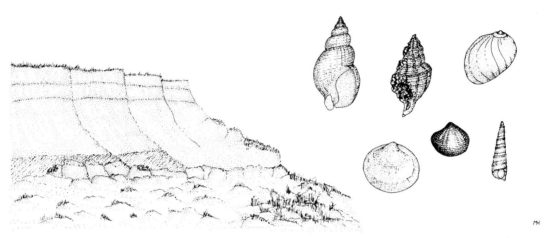

Fossil molluscs from the red crag cliffs at Walton-on-the-Naze. The large whelk spirals in the opposite direction to present-day whelks. (MH)

thistles and knotted hedge parsley are two species more or less restricted to seawalls as is the squirrel-tail grass. The seawall soil is well drained and covered with (often tussocky) grass. Warmed by the sun, seawalls make good haunts for animals not suited to the waterlogged marshes. Adders are fairly common. Rabbits burrow into the wall, hares make their forms amongst the long grass and field voles are abundant amongst the grass tussocks.

Sometimes the field voles undergo a population explosion and become common over wide areas of marshland. Many predatory birds and mammals find field voles ideal food. They often form the main item in bird of prey pellets, and foxes definitely prefer them to bank voles and woodmice, if they have the choice. Short-eared owls are rare breeding birds on Essex marshes but regular winter visitors. They tend to congregate when small mammals, especially voles, are abundant. That this has always been so is delightfully recorded by Holinshed in his *Chronicles* four hundred years ago:

'About Hallowtide last past (1580), in the marshes of Danesie Hundred, in a place called Southminster, in the Countie of Essex, a strange thing happened: there suddenlie appeared an infinite multitude of mice, which, overwhelming the whole earth in the said marshes, did sheare and gnaw the grasse by the roots, spoiling and tainting the same with their venemous teeth, in such sort that the cattell which grased thereon were smitten with a murreine, and died thereof; which vermin by policie of man could not be destroied, till now at last it came to passe that there flocked together all about the same marshes such a number of owles as all the shire was not able to yield; whereby the marsh holders were shortly delivered from the vexation of the said mice.'

The mice were voles, the owls short-eared and the farmers (as they still do) exaggerated the damage done by wildlife: voles' teeth are not venomous.

At the time Holinshed was writing, the coastal marshes were valued mainly as sheep grazing — as they had been since Domesday. Domesday Book records grazing for 18,000 sheep on coastal pastures. The pasture lands were so valuable that rights to them were split up amongst many inland parishes. It was not until the mid-16th century that Foulness, for example, became a parish in its own right.

The grazing could be enlarged by building new seawalls further out on the saltmarsh. The remains of the old seawalls are low banks crossing the grazing marsh, and form the sub-habitat richest in plant species. The rabbit holes in these inland banks form one of the most favoured breeding sites for shelduck.

The construction of a seawall leaves a deep dyke on the inland side: these borrow-dykes fill with (usually brackish) water and have their own characteristic plants. Two species of tasselweed — the beaked and the rarer spiral type — are found there, along with the marine water crowfoot, which can stand up to 1.2% salinity, and the fat duckweed. Other dykes and ditches cross the marshes. Traditionally these are cleared every 7-10 years to maintain them for drainage. The clearance helps wildlife by maintaining a mix of open water, just cleared, and parts due for clearing, almost choked with reeds. Sea club rush is often common in the brackish dykes, and common reed abundant in the freshwater and brackish ones alike. Reed warblers breed amongst them and, in one borrow-dyke reedbed, is the only Essex breeding colony of the bearded reedling. Coot and moorhens are also common in the dykes. In late summer, mud is exposed in the dykes and attracts common and green sandpipers together with an occasional wood sandpiper.

As well as the drainage dykes, wider expanses of freshwater occur where seawalls have cut off a once tidal channel from the sea. The result is a 'fleet'. The fleets and dykes are of greatest interest for their rare aquatic insects. Great silver water beetles can still be found and there are many species of dragonfly and damselfly. These need fairly fresh water and cannot survive flooding by the sea. The dainty damselfly had its only British breeding population in a marshland pond near Hadleigh. It became extinct in Britain when the 1953 Great Tide flooded the pond. Another species, once more widespread, had not been seen in Britain since 1971, until it was rediscovered at two sites in Essex in 1983. In both cases this rarity (the scarce emerald damselfly) was breeding in a dyke almost choked with sea club-rush. This, and the many commoner species of dragonfly, are likely to survive in these dykes and ditches until the marshes are ploughed and agricultural runoff makes the water unsuitable for most dragonflies.

Where the grass is left ungrazed, it grows up into a rich community bright with flowers and butterflies. Most of the butterflies are widespread species like common blues, meadow browns and the Essex skipper — a species discovered in Essex but by no means restricted to the county. In a few tiny areas in the Rochford Hundred the last Essex populations of marbled whites struggle to survive.

The beautiful cream-spot tiger moth is a mainly coastal species, as are several other moths with a strong south-easterly bias to their British distribution. Grasshoppers are abundant and their relatives, Roesel's bush-cricket and the short-winged cone-head, are especially associated with Essex coastal grasslands. The bush-cricket is especially easy to spot in late summer, when the adult males sing a continuous high-pitched buzzing song.

The plants differ depending on whether the marsh has lime-rich (alkaline) soils or is fairly neutral. The Foulness marshes are lime-rich and boast the slender hare's ear, slender bird's-foot trefoil, sea clover with its delicate pink flowers, and Borrer's saltmarsh grass — a localised grass that seems to specialise in growing in cattle hoof-prints. The neutral grasslands of the Blackwater area have been almost entirely ploughed up and their flowering plants lost.

The commonest breeding bird of the grazing marsh is the skylark, one of the few species that will remain to breed when the marsh is ploughed. In the low lying, wetter pastures — another of the important sub-habitats — redshank and lapwing still breed. Kestrels, the main bird of prey, breed mostly on the pylons with which the CEGB has decorated most of the wide open landscapes of Essex.

To the west of Canvey Island, the Thames-side grazing marshes have mostly been replaced with heavy industry, chemical stores, power stations, rubbish dumps and dredgings from the river. Except to the selective eye of the bird-watcher, the area is an eyesore, but it does have considerable natural history interest.

Rainham marsh contains some of the last remnants of upper Thames marsh. In the early 1960s the Port of London Authority created special lagoons in which to dump dredged mud. The lost grasslands became wetlands, where oystercatchers and ringed plovers breed and winter flocks of waders feed. When the mud pumped into the lagoons dries, small pools appear and a varied vegetation returns. On other parts of the marsh, rubbish tipping attracts large flocks of gulls to feed on the rubbish direct, and other flocks of swallows and martins to feed on the insects rising from the decaying rubbish. On much of the marsh, an army firing range protects the wildlife from too much disturbance.

Between the river Ingrebourne and the Ford works, the remains of Hornchurch marsh have been improved, from a bird-watcher's point of view, by the construction of a sewage works. The filter beds and settling lagoons attract feeding duck, swallows and martins.

The scrub on derelict areas, near the factories, provides the major breeding sites for stonechats. In 1890, stonechats were recorded as common on 'furze-covered commons throughout the county'. In 1974 a modern ornithologist described the new breeding habitat: 'Amongst a jungle of rubble . . . a stonechat hops furtively from barbed wire fence to rusty boiler against the imperious backcloth of factory complexes'.

Oystercatcher pair nesting inside seawall. (RH)

ABOVE: A typical Essex seawall: right, the outside with a creek at the top of a saltmarsh; left, the inside with a borrow dyke filled with common reeds. (DC) BELOW: The seawall which separates Two Tree island from Leigh Marsh: a wild area close to the Southend conurbation at the mouth of the Thames estuary. (TI) OPPOSITE LEFT: Common reeds in a borrow dyke. (RG) RIGHT: A hen harrier hunts over Ramsey Marsh near the Blackwater estuary. (RG) BELOW: High tide floods the causeway leading to Skippers Island nature reserve. (TI).

OPPOSITE ABOVE: The Walton cliffs: the only true cliffs in Essex. (TI) BELOW: Brent geese have now taken to feeding on farm fields. (RG) ABOVE LEFT: Redshank nest, hidden among long grass. (HMcS) RIGHT: Brown-tail moth caterpillars in their nest. (DH) BELOW LEFT: The scarce emerald damselfly was rediscovered, as a British species, in Essex, in 1983. (EB) RIGHT: The Essex skipper is distinguished from the small skipper by the black tips to its antennae. (EB)

ABOVE: Fisher's estuarine moth — a species found nowhere in Britain except the Hamford Water area of Essex. (PEM) LEFT: Roessel's bush-cricket is especially associated with Essex coastal regions. (EB) RIGHT: Great green bush-crickets are the largest of the bush-crickets and are found most frequently near the coast. (EB)

Forests and Woodlands

Old pollards in Epping Forest. (JF)

'Wildwood' is an evocative name for the original, natural woodland that grew all over Essex in the few thousand years between the end of the ice age and the start of the period when man became the dominant influence on woodland development. The name was coined by Dr Oliver Rackham, whose brilliant combination of historical and archaeological detective work with present-day field work, has led to a massive growth in knowledge of ancient woodlands in East Anglia. Much of the factual information that follows has come from his published works.

Between about 7500 and 5000 BC, all of Essex that was not wetland was woodland. The freshwater marshes and coastal saltings would have been much more extensive than today but, even so, the wildwood must have covered at least 85% of Essex. No unaltered wildwood survives anywhere in Europe let alone Essex; to know what this prehistoric woodland was like it is necessary to search in peaty ground for fossil pollen. Each year, trees produce a mass of pollen grains and, with a microscope, it is fairly easy to identify the species of tree from which a pollen grain has come. When pollen grains fall into boggy ground they are preserved along with the developing peat deposit. So, by examining peat, and allowing for the fact that trees of different species produce different amounts of pollen, it is possible to deduce the mix of trees in the wildwood at the time the peat was laid down. The technique of 'carbon-dating' will reveal how old the peat is.

The only suitable peat deposits in Essex, that have been examined by students of the wildwood, are in Epping Forest and the Lea Valley. The valley woodland, in water-logged soil, had a high proportion of sallow and alder trees, as wet woodlands still do today. On the dry ground of the Epping Forest ridge, the wildwood was a diverse mixture: very different from today's Epping Forest but fairly similar to the wildwood elsewhere in East Anglia. Small-leaved lime was by far the commonest tree, a species now quite absent from the Forest but still found in some ancient coppice woodlands in the north of Essex. Chalkney Wood is one of the best lime woods in the county.

Oak was the second most common tree of the Epping wildwood, with beech in third place. These two species are still in the top three trees in the Forest and have been joined by hornbeam: a great rarity in the wildwood days. Epping Forest was unusual, amongst East Anglian wildwoods, in having so much beech — this species was probably much rarer in northern Essex, as it still is today. Hazel came fourth in wildwood Epping; today it is a great rarity in the forest but common in most coppice woodlands. The remaining native trees of Epping Forest included a small amount of pine, birch and elm. Elm and ash are likely to have been more important parts of the wildwood in some other areas of Essex.

59

The conversion of the wildwood, a continuous tract of woodland over the whole of dry Essex, into numerous, mainly small, woods that today cover just under 4% of Essex, is a process that began in the stone age. Mesolithic man was a hunter in the wildwood rather than a cultivator of cleared ground. It is possible that his use of fire, to drive game from the woodland, hastened the decline of the pine. Coniferous trees, as the Forestry Commission knows to its cost, are the only trees that burn easily while still standing.

Neolithic and bronze age man, from 3100 to 800 BC, really began the transformation of the wildwood. Much of the earliest clearing was of freely draining soil on the higher ground. The fertility of this soil would have been rather quickly exhausted, and would have been allowed to develop into heathland and secondary woodland. This almost certainly happened in Epping Forest: the iron age encampments at Ambresbury Banks and Loughton Camp imply that, at that time, the area was quite open enough to spot enemies from some distance. Both the Epping and Danbury ridges have, at the present time, small amounts of heathland and much woodland on their gravelly soils.

The later part of the iron age and the Roman period saw a tremendous phase of woodland clearance, with improved ploughs allowing cultivation of nearly all soil types. In a period of 700 years about half the woodland had gone. Roman Essex is believed to have had at least 50% farmland, and much of the woodland near to farm settlements would already have come under coppice management, being repeatedly cut to produce firewood and fencing materials.

The Domesday survey of 1086 provides the first good historical record of the distribution of woodlands in Essex, although it is a record that is more difficult to interpret than for some counties. This is because Essex is a 'swine-county': instead of recording Essex woodlands by area, William the Conqueror's assessors tallied each wood in terms of how many pigs it could support. Since annual variations in acorn crops meant that the real number of pigs in a woodland must often have been different from the theoretical number recorded for taxation purposes, estimating the area of Essex woodland in 1086 is not easy. To compound the difficulties, coppice woodland produces less food for pigs than unmanaged woodland. What is certain is that Essex was, in those days, a well-wooded county. Three-quarters of Essex settlements had woodlands: a higher proportion than any county except Hertfordshire. To the north, Suffolk was more densely populated and had much less woodland. A glance at Dr Rackham's map of woodland in Domesday Essex shows clearly that the Epping Forest area and much of central-south Essex was then, as now, well wooded. The coastal area had little woodland, and a band of land running from Maldon to the north of Chelmsford and west to Sawbridgeworth had no large woods. This band still separates northern Essex with its ancient coppice woods, from southern Essex with large areas of woodland concentrated on gravel ridges between the cultivated valleys.

The Domesday map also shows that, in the north-western quarter of Essex, nearly all the larger woods had declined in pig-feeding capacity in the 20 years since the Battle of Hastings. This indicates active woodland clearance and an intensification of coppice management in that part of Essex where almost all present-day woods are derived from ancient coppices.

As village settlements grew and fragmented the wildwood, uncleared areas of wildwood were left, often on the boundary between settlements, as a source of the woodland products that every village needed. Most villagers would have had rights to cut firewood, fencing stakes and wood for binding thatch. Repeated cutting of the trees at ground level, and their subsequent regrowth, produced the huge coppice stools characteristic of ancient coppices. Regrowth was only successful if browsing stock was kept out of the wood after coppicing work: so coppice woods have a clear boundary with a ditch and bank. The lord of the manor had the right to mature trees of adequate size for building purposes. He would ensure that coppicing did not remove his standard (timber) trees and that adequate numbers of replacement standards were allowed to grow on. Standard trees in coppice woods were almost always oaks; not because they were the most common tree in the original wildwood, but because their timber was the most highly valued for building houses, and the acorn crop fed pigs.

There was no single species of tree favoured for coppicing. The mix of trees in an ancient coppice reflects those species that occurred naturally in the area and which could survive repeated coppicing. The main exception to this rule is sweet chestnut, a non-native tree introduced to Essex at least as long ago as Roman times: chestnut wood and charcoal have been identified at Roman sites in Essex. The ancient chestnut coppices in eastern Essex may have been planted, or the species may have spread naturally after its introduction. Chestnut coppice tends to be more valuable than other species and is likely to have been encouraged. Chestnut only does well on acid soils and all the Essex chestnut coppices are in eastern Essex, away from the chalky boulder clay. Norsey Wood, Billericay and Copperas Wood on the Stour estuary are two good examples of ancient chestnut coppice where coppicing is continued today for conservation reasons. Many other woods in these parts of Essex are hornbeam coppices. Thrift Wood at Bicknacre is a good example of a hornbeam coppice now managed by the ENT.

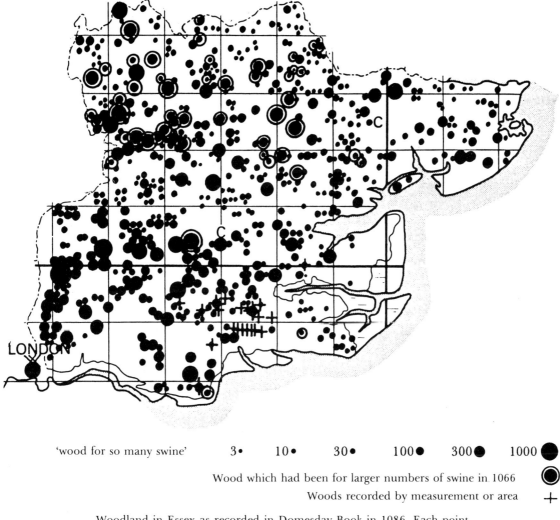

'wood for so many swine'   3 •   10 •   30 •   100 ●   300 ●   1000 ●

Wood which had been for larger numbers of swine in 1066   ◉

Woods recorded by measurement or area   +

Woodland in Essex as recorded in Domesday Book in 1086. Each point represents one mention of woodland. (From a map by Oliver Rackham in *Ancient Woodland*).

61

The conservation importance of coppice woods is twofold. First, virtually all Essex coppices are primary woodland: they have had a continuity of woodland cover from the days of the wildwood until the present time. They have never been cleared and ploughed — although they may have been clear felled and allowed to regrow. This means that woodland plant (and some animal) species which are poor at colonising new, secondary, woodland will survive only in the primary woods. And this brings us to the second point of importance: many woodland flowers are not only restricted to primary woodlands but flower best in the conditions created by coppicing.

The coppice cycle, that is the time allowed between one wood-cutting and the next, has tended to increase over the centuries. Cycles as short as four or five years, recorded from the 13th century, can have produced little but bundles of twigs. Since 1600, nearly all cycles have been between ten and twenty years, although abandoned coppices have been recoppiced after a forty or fifty year gap with no long-term loss of wildlife interest.

The original wildwood had a mixed age tree canopy, with plenty of open areas where trees had recently fallen, that would have allowed light to the ground flora. In woods that are cut, trees grow more densely and shade out the ground flora, except in the years immediately following coppicing, when the ground flora can grow and bloom freely. While coppice woods are in no way natural habitats, they not only mimic some aspects of the wildwood but have existed almost as long. Some woods have been coppiced since Roman times and have had nearly 2,000 years to adjust to this pattern of management: that compares with only 2,500 years when natural, fully developed, wildwood existed undisturbed in post-ice-age, pre-neolithic Essex.

In a county with almost no truly natural habitats, environments with a stable pattern of management and a rich diversity of wildlife are of great conservation importance, even if not natural. That is why the Nature Conservancy Council recognises ancient coppice woods as amongst the most important of inland Essex habitats.

Oliver Rackham has investigated over 160 ancient Essex woodlands — all with a documented history of at least 280 years and a select few with written records surviving from pre-Domesday times. Over a quarter of these woods have been partly or completely grubbed out since the war, and many of the remainder have been replanted with conifers. In February 1984 the Ministry of Agriculture gave figures to Parliament showing that 931 hectares of ancient Essex woodland had been totally cleared in the last 50 years. Essex has lost a larger area than any of the other 20 counties for which figures were given. At first sight, it is difficult to see how this rate of destruction can tally with figures provided by the Forestry Commission, which show that Essex has about 15,000 hectares of woodland: a slight increase since the turn of the century. The apparent increase in woodland is a product of a changed survey technique (smaller areas are now counted as woods than in previous surveys) and a genuine increase in secondary woodlands that occurred during the 1930s agricultural depression.

To identify a wood as real ancient woodland it is easier, and almost as reliable, to look for the presence of certain woodland flowers, as it is to search diligently through masses of historical records. These indicator species are plants that cannot colonise new woodland across open ground — although, very slowly, they may invade secondary woodland that directly adjoins a primary wood.

In the chalky boulder clay region of north-west Essex, the best indicator species is the oxlip. In the whole of Britain, oxlips are confined to this soil type in Essex and the adjacent regions of Cambridgeshire and Suffolk. Oxlips look rather like a cross between a primrose and a cowslip, and this is what some botanists thought they were when first discovered in Essex. It was the great Epping naturalist, Henry Doubleday, who produced convincing proof that they were a true species. He pointed out that the majority of oxlip woods have no primroses at all and that cowslips prefer drier ground outside woods. He also raised oxlips from seed and showed that they bred true, with no reversions to cowslip or primrose types, as expected if the oxlip was a hybrid.

Oxlips are found in all the coppice woods on the chalky boulder clay and most woods in this area consist of some mix of hazel, ash and maple coppice. Part of Hales Wood, now mainly converted to conifers, has been preserved as a national nature reserve on the grounds that it is a good, typical example of an oxlip wood. Today, thanks to more active coppice management, the ENT nature reserves at Shadwell Wood and West Wood have even better displays of oxlips.

In the 1970s it was estimated that the Hempstead Wood, a privately owned SSSI woodland, had more oxlips than any other wood: about three-quarters of a million plants. Now that half the wood had been coniferized by the Forestry Commission and much of the remainder left uncoppiced, the oxlips are in decline. The large population of deer, which have a predilection for oxlips, has probably contributed to the loss.

Oxlip woods have a rich variety of other woodland flowers. The strange herb paris is usually present and is another firm indicator of ancient woodland, as are the greater butterfly and early purple orchids.

The delicate wood anemones and wood sorrels are found in ancient coppices on most soil types. Wood anemones, in particular, do well on acid or water-logged soils or in the shadier parts of a coppice. There are especially good displays of them in the ENT nature reserves at Thrift Wood, Moat Wood and the Danbury complex of woods.

Lily-of-the-valley is another speciality of the Danbury complex of woods and is also found in some other south Essex woods on freely draining soil. Bluebells are widespread and found in a majority of Essex woods, although woods where the bluebells form a complete carpet over a wide area are less common. Weeleyhall Wood and Blakes Wood are two of the ENT's best bluebell nature reserves. Possibly as many as ten million bluebells flowered in Blakes Wood in 1983. Bluebell carpets of this magnitude are a particular feature of British woods: the species is much rarer across the Channel.

Primroses are absent from most of the oxlip woods and do not tend to grow in hedges and roadside banks as they do in western England. The major primrose woods are in the Rodings area and the group of small-leaved lime woods to the north of Coggeshall. The best remaining part of Chalkney Wood has been protected by Essex County Council as a public amenity wood. Markshall Wood covered 160 hectares and half this area was lime: probably the largest single area of lime woodland in Britain. Unfortunately, when the late owner of much of Markshall left his woods for the benefit of the nation, the lime area was largely destroyed by Forestry Commission replanting.

While medieval lords and villagers were extending and consolidating the coppice management of small Essex woods, the Norman kings introduced new laws that were to have a great effect on the larger tracts of woodland. The forest laws were concerned with regulating hunting and timber felling, or at least providing the king with a tax-income levied by fining the transgressors.

Forest law originally covered most of Essex but by 1300 had been restricted to four large areas. These legal forests were not solid woodland: they were normal inhabited areas, farmed in the usual way but subject to special laws. Within each legal forest was at least one area of large physical forest containing the king's deer and trees. Usually the physical forest was on poor agricultural land and survived even when kings lost interest in maintaining their forest laws and courts.

Royal forests were an important feature of many remote and upland regions, but Essex is unusual in having had four royal forests in a well populated region close to London. It is the only one of the home counties with any such forests. The largest of the forests was in the south-west, adjoining London's East End, and includes the physical forests of Epping, Wintry and Hainault. Local commoners enjoyed rights to graze their animals and lop wood, while timber oaks and deer remained Crown property.

It is the combination of grazing and wood-cutting that has produced the special character of Epping Forest: an uncompartmented wood-pasture. Cattle were free to graze anywhere and would have prevented the regrowth of lopped trees were it not for the practice of pollarding: cutting the trees above the reach of browsing animals. The Forest became a mixture of open heathy plains, wet grasslands and open woodland, where enough light reached the forest floor to permit a good cover of ground plants. Wood-pastures do not have carpets of spring flowers as these are sensitive to grazing and trampling pressures. Nevertheless, Epping Forest contained a rich diversity of ground plants plus an interesting range of lichens and ferns growing as epiphytes on the pollard trees.

In one of the earliest examples of a successful conservation campaign, Epping Forest was, in 1878, rescued from imminent destruction by enclosure and clearing, and given into the care of the Corporation of the City of London. The present Epping Forest covers about 2,400 hectares and includes Wintry Forest to the north of Epping. Much of the Forest land is open grassland and public sports grounds, but over half the area is woodland: the largest and most important block of ancient woodland anywhere near London. The Nature Conservancy Council regards it as a grade 2 SSSI (which still means it is of national importance) and it would probably have been graded in the top category had air pollution not removed most of the lichens and public pressure damaged the more sensitive vegetation.

The conservators of Epping Forest have a difficult task; indeed the Act of Parliament that saved the Forest probably gave them an impossible set of conflicting tasks and objectives. Limited ecological knowledge was a problem in the early days, to be replaced now with a lack of money, and limited manpower, which has to be split between the conflicting needs of organised sport, horse riding, general visitors by car and on foot, and nature conservation.

The structure of Epping woodland has changed dramatically following the virtual cessation of pollarding in 1878. With regular pollarding, trees can grow quite close together without competing for light. With no more pollarding, the old trunks put forth new, massive branches that struggle up towards the light, producing a dense even-aged canopy to the new high forest. The ground layer lost its vegetation and became just a layer of dead leaves — pleasant to walk through, but lacking its previous diversity of wildlife.

Pollard trees, like coppice stools, are virtually immortal so long as the regular cutting is continued. Without repollarding, the tree is doomed in about a century. So, at the present time; Epping Forest is losing many of its old pollards.The doom can take one of three forms. The tree may lose the race for the light. This has happened to many of the pollarded oaks, which have been overtopped by faster growing beeches and have died in the shade. The second fate is for the tree to outgrow its strength. Pollarding does render the tree long-lived, but at the price of having a pollard boll which traps water and the old trunk tends to rot internally. This does not matter as long as the trunk has little weight to support: and the water-filled rot holes even have an interesting insect fauna of their own. Zoologists have found Epping Forest tree holes to be the breeding site of a rare mosquito *(Orthopodomyia)*. As the new trunks grow atop the old rotten pollard, the weight increases. Finally the tree breaks apart under its own weight.

The third fate affects mainly the beech pollards: they are a shallow rooted species well adapted to grow on shallow soils. That is why they are so common on the gravel deposits of the High Beech area (and may explain the survival of both spellings of the place name: the high beeches grow on elevated gravel deposits — a high beach). As the beeches grow tall, a high wind can easily topple them, and many have fallen in recent years. The rate of loss of beech trees increased following the drought of 1976, when many trees failed to draw in enough water through their shallow roots.

One of the best features of the management of Epping Forest is that trees are not planted. Instead, natural regeneration is relied upon, and natural methods have produced an abundance (some would say a super-abundance) of new saplings. Birch quickly colonises wherever the falling of a beech creates a clearing. Birch is also invading the heathland areas — a cause for concern since heathlands have become so rare. Oak does not regenerate in the shade of other trees, but successfully invades the grass and scrub areas at the edge of the wood. Beech can grow from seed within the shade of the woodland and after a good beechmast year the forest floor is a carpet of beech seedlings. In the more open areas they survive to produce a thicket of saplings some of which will be the majestic trees our great-grandchildren will admire.

Whether there will also be historic and interesting pollards for those great-grandchildren is another matter. Woodmans' Glade and an area near the Conservation Centre have been experimentally repollarded. Many people feel that pollarding should be reintroduced on a wider basis, to maintain the historic and wildlife interest of a real medieval wood-pasture.

red stag   fallow buck   roebuck   muntjac buck

Four species of deer now breed in Essex woods; both sexes have the distinctive markings on rump and tail but only the males have antlers.
(CA)

Hatfield Forest was managed in a rather different way from Epping. It is a compartmented forest: its defined and embanked woodlands could be closed to the grazing animals while they regrew after coppicing. Pollarding was restricted to the open areas. Under the management of the National Trust, Hatfield retains almost all of its medieval features. To quote Oliver Rackham: 'Hatfield is the only place where one can step back into the Middle Ages to see, with only a small effort of imagination, what a Forest looked like in use'.

The other Essex forests have suffered various fates. Kingswood passed into private ownership in the 16th century and hardly a trace of it survives, although a few small lime woods to the north of

Colchester may once have been part of it. Hainault was enclosed in 1851 and within a few weeks 92% of the woodland had gone. It is now farmland or housing, except the small section which is managed as an access woodland by the GLC. Ecologically it is like a small version of Epping Forest.

Writtle Forest is the least known and perhaps the most interesting. It was a compartmented forest but, a reverse of the Hatfield design, had the woods in the middle and the plains at the edge. Mill Green Common is a surviving part of the plain. Most of the extensive woods between Blackmore and Margaretting were part of Writtle Forest. Edney Common and part of Edney Woods have been destroyed for farming, but most of the features of the old Forest remain. Again to quote Oliver Rackham: 'Nearly everything one sees there is of fourteenth century or earlier: the great assart surrounded by hornbeam springs and alder glades: the heathland, pollard oaks, and wood-banks; the lonely cottage, with a palfrey grazing in its pightle, on the site of the hermitage where a solitary monk dwelt. This astonishing survival from the depths of the medieval countryside is within twenty five miles of St Paul's Cathedral'. What is almost equally astonishing, and rather sad, is that the Nature Conservancy Council has not designated even a tiny part of this important forest as an SSSI.

Writtle Forest is cut in two by Writtle Deer Park, founded in the early 13th century. The King's deer lived at large in the forest but a nobleman, or rich commoner, kept his deer in a park. Oliver Rackham has traced records of 159 Essex parks dating from before 1535 — more than any other county so far investigated. They were not just used for deer but were sources of wood, timber and pasture just like the unenclosed forests.

By the late 19th century there were only ten parks still containing deer: in most cases these were fallow deer although a few also contained red or roe — species native to Essex. Fallow deer are introductions, although of long standing: probably they were brought into Essex in early Norman times and soon became the main object of the chase in royal forests as well as the main parkland species.

Of the ten deer parks surviving to 1892, only one still has deer. That is Quendon Park, which contains a large herd of fallow. It is a private park that has recently been sold to a secretive foreign investor, rumoured locally to be the Sultan of Oman. Three new deer parks have been created during this century: Bedfords Park is public and has a few red deer, St Osyth Priory is private and has both red and fallow, while the newest park is the so-called 'Deer Sanctuary' adjacent to Epping Forest.

The Epping Forest fallow deer are mostly of the dark colour variety. The wild herd, which numbered two to three hundred in the early part of this century, was declining rapidly in the 1950s and 1960s. Increasing human disturbance, loss of dense undergrowth where the deer could lie-up, and road accidents, were all problems for the deer. The 44 hectare sanctuary at Birch Hall was created in the 1960s. In the best medieval tradition, a deer-proof fence was erected, deer jumps provided to let the deer in and out and then, when the deer were in, the jumps were closed. In the safety of the sanctuary the herd has increased to over a hundred and is now culled to keep numbers in check. In the Forest proper, the deer have dwindled to the point of extinction as a breeding species, although wanderers are still seen.

Ironically, while Epping Forest deer were in decline, wild deer in most of the rest of Essex were increasing rapidly. Most of the remaining deer parks were disbanded during the second war and many of the deer escaped into the countryside. After the war, a combination of new conifer plantations, and declining numbers of agricultural employees and woodsmen, provided good cover and lack of disturbance for the deer. Not only have the feral fallow deer become widespread, but they have been joined by three other species. Small muntjac deer, introduced from China via Woburn Abbey, escaped and arrived in Essex by 1941. Today they are widespread and abundant, even wandering well into urban areas.

Red and roe deer are true natives of Essex but the last wild ones in Epping Forest disappeared long ago. They were reintroduced in the latter part of the 19th century, the red being deliberately removed soon after, because they became a nuisance. The roe eventually became extinct, again, in the 1920s. Happily both species are now back in Essex, having arrived naturally in the mid-1960s by spreading south from their haunts in the extensive East Anglian forests. Both species now live and breed in the Forestry Commission's plantations of Walden Forest and are sometimes seen in other north Essex woodlands.

Essex red deer grow considerably larger than deer in the Scottish highlands. At the time of the autumn rut, the roaring and fighting stags are a magnificent, and a somewhat frightening spectacle. The return of Britain's largest land animal to breed in such a densely populated county as Essex is an event worth celebrating: it is due mainly to the habitats created by the Forestry Commission.

Woodland in present-day Essex. (Drawn by KA for *The Flora of Essex*).

Unlike Suffolk and Norfolk, where huge tracts of heathland have been planted with conifers to form major new forests, Essex Forestry Commission woods have been converted to conifers from ancient coppice woodlands. Most of this coniferization was carried out during the 1950s and early 1960s and was the cause of much adverse comment. In the early years the Forestry Commission certainly gave every impression of having little regard for wildlife: for example ancient coppices were sometimes sprayed from the air with chemical defoliants to prepare the way for coniferization. Botanists rightly point out that dense conifer plantations let little light reach the ground and the once rich flora of the old coppice woodlands is doomed in a plantation. But there are compensations for this loss — not least being the fact that had the woods not become Forestry Commission plantations they would almost certainly have been grubbed out and turned into arable deserts. Wide rides are created in plantation woodlands to act as firebreaks and to permit access by large vehicles. Under recent, sympathetic management these have become superb wildlife reserves. Usually the original trees and shrubs are left as coppiced shrubs along the edge of the rides. The rides themselves, unenriched by farm fertilisers and colonised by much of the ancient woodland flora, became the most diverse of all grassland environments in Essex. Open, sunny, flower-rich rides are the perfect habitat for butterflies and the Forestry Commission woodlands have a greater number and variety of butterflies than most other Essex woods.

There are about 900 hectares of Forestry Commission plantation in Essex — this amount is declining as, under Government direction, the Commission is selling off some of its outlying woodlands. The major areas that will be retained are the large collection of woods in the Saffron Walden area, known collectively as Walden Forest, and the north central woodlands in the Markshall area. Most of the large woods have free public access and the rides make delightful walks — but in some woods shooting syndicates have the right to exclude the public.

Great Bendysh Wood is an interesting example of a Forestry Commission wood in Walden Forest. It was designated an SSSI before it was coniferized. Now, in its new plantation form, it is the only wood in which all four species of Essex deer are known to breed. Its rides are bright with orchids — a higher density of spotted orchids and greater butterfly orchids than the neighbouring nature reserves can boast. At the edge of the rides all the ancient woodland indicator plants, such as herb paris, still survive, although in reduced numbers. In the dark depths of the wood, the needle carpet is bare of flowers except the rare birds-nest orchid, a saprophyte which has no green leaves and so needs no light. On an early summer evening, turtle doves call and, occasionally, woodcock make their roding flights. There are few woods in Essex where woodcock breed and a roding male is the first sign of attempted breeding. And yet, despite this rich variety of wildlife, the Nature Conservancy Council is planning to delete Great Bendysh from its list of SSSIs, because coniferization has reduced its scientific interest.

The present total of conifer plantation in Essex is 16% of all woods — a lesser proportion than in some counties. Provided they increase no further, the conifer plantations can probably be regarded as an asset, rather than a total loss to wildlife. The present total includes private woods whose owners have taken advantage of Government subsidies and tax reliefs and converted their woodlands to conifers. This is a continuing source of loss and a real threat to some of the county's surviving ancient woodland.

The variety of woodland structure, produced by the various patterns of woodland management, produces a corresponding variety in woodland bird populations. Epping Forest is a favoured haunt for the hawfinch, which nests in old pollards. Nuthatches, too, like the Forest with its absence of dense undergrowth. Nightingales, in contrast, need a sunlit scrub zone in which to nest and search for insects. They have gone from the Forest but survive in the coppice nature reserves of north and central Essex.

The nightingale is one of several summer migrants that have declined across the whole country. Whitethroats and redstarts are two others, and the wryneck has become extinct as a breeding species. In all these cases, it is likely that problems in the birds' winter range, or on migration, such as the expansion of the Sahara desert into the Sahel region, are responsible for the declines.

Some resident species have increased in numbers; a good example is the redpoll, which has become a common breeding species in Epping and Hainault Forests and, in winter, flocks of over 500 birds have been recorded in these and other mature woodlands.

Birds that nest in hollow trees are especially associated with parkland, where ancient trees are allowed to remain for a centuries' long senescence. Little owls, stock doves and jackdaws are three parkland tree-hole nesters. Conifer woods, low on tree holes, provide a different range of habitats. The tiny goldcrest, a conifer specialist, has increased in recent years.

The sparrowhawk still hangs on as a breeding species in a central Essex wood. It suffered gamekeeper persecution in Victorian times, as did all birds of prey. This same persecution eliminated pine martens, wildcats and polecats from Essex woods. The predatory birds suffered a second decline in the 1950s to early 1970s when DDT usage was at its height. With both legal protection and less toxic insecticides in use, there must be hope that some of our woodland birds of prey will make a comeback.

A major nocturnal predator, and by far the commonest owl in Essex, is the tawny owl. It breeds in the great majority of Essex woods. Tawny owls hunt mainly for small rodents — the bank voles and woodmice which, in Essex as in every wood in Britain, are abundant. Interestingly, it was in Essex, in 1832, that the bank vole was discovered as a British species. Previously it had been confused with the field vole and this same confusion persisted into this century. It is now known that bank voles are extremely common, probably more so than the field voles which always avoid woodlands.

Woodmice and bank voles feed mainly at ground level, or amongst low bushes. The woodland canopy is home to several climbing rodents. Squirrels, of course, have undergone a change of colour. The introduced grey squirrel spread into Essex comparatively late, hindered, it is believed, by the barrier of the Lea Valley. There were a few pre-war reports and during the war the greys colonised Epping Forest. By 1960 almost the whole of Essex was occupied and now the invasion is complete. In some small woods, red squirrels survived only a few years after the greys arrived, but elsewhere they co-existed for up to 25 years. Today the red is extinct in Essex.

The nocturnal climbing rodents are more secretive than squirrels and are true native species still. Dormice are restricted mainly to the coppice woods and are often found in nature reserves nesting in the bird-boxes. The yellow-necked mouse, larger than the similar woodmouse, is widespread in all sorts of Essex woods and quite often climbs into the lofts of country houses.

One of the least understood and saddest losses has been the decline and extinction of so many woodland butterflies. The most spectacular decline has been in the fritillary butterflies that, in the caterpillar stage, feed on woodland violets. Five species (small pearl-bordered, pearl-bordered, high brown, dark green and silver-washed) all bred in Essex between the wars. The small pearl-bordered declined in the 1930s and the rest in the 1940s and 1950s. All are now extinct as breeding species, although occasional vagrants are spotted and a recolonisation is not impossible. The heath fritillary, the most endangered butterfly in Britain, became extinct in Essex at the end of the 19th century. It was successfully reintroduced into Belfairs and Hockley Woods and survived from 1925 to the early 1970s. Now a further reintroduction is being attempted at another site in Essex where the caterpillars' foodplant, cow-wheat, grows plentifully.

Of the other woodland species that bred in Essex this century, the Duke of Burgundy fritillary disappeared in 1924 but the white admiral survives in a few woods in the extreme north-east. Interestingly, the purple emperor and the brown hairstreak, both known from Epping Forest in the 19th century but not seen there since 1900, were found again in the Forest during 1983. Whether these exciting records are a real recolonisation, or escaped captive specimens, remains to be seen.

The one butterfly that is expanding its range in Essex is the speckled wood. Almost absent in 1900, it has spread back into the county from the south-east and is now found everywhere except the extreme north-west.

There are well over a thousand species of beetles in Essex and some are just as clear an indicator of an ancient woodland as are certain woodland flowers. Epping Forest is by far the best beetle wood in the county, and not just because it has been the most closely investigated by expert entomologists. What Epping Forest has in plenty are dead and dying trees that are left to rot where they fall. This is vitally important for many beetles that live only in decaying wood. Perhaps the most spectacular species is the stag beetle, whose larva burrows for several years in the trunk of a dying tree before it hatches as an adult. Stag beetles are found in many Essex woods and parklands. Other species are much less widespread: of the over 1,300 species of beetle found in Epping Forest, 196 have been seen nowhere else in Essex.

Each autumn for the last century, members of the Essex Field Club have collected fungi in Epping Forest on the annual 'Fungus Foray'. At the last published count, just over 700 species of basidiomycete fungi (the larger type of fungi that include the normal mushrooms and toadstools) had been recorded. Scarcely a year goes by without a new species being discovered in the Forest. Epping Forest is famous for fungi — but fungi are an important part of every woodland community. Not only do they rot the dead wood (and kill living trees) but many species form symbiotic associations with living trees. These fungus/tree roots 'co-operatives' are called mycorrhizae and are essential for the growth of most tree species.

The classic 'toadstool' — the red and white marked fly agaric — is common in Epping Forest wherever birch trees grow. It is fairly poisonous but not as deadly as its close relation, the death cap — also common in the Forest. It is the presence of these, and other poisonous species, that makes most people wary of collecting the many delicious edible fungi in the Forest.

Most birch trees will die as a result of infection by the birch bracket fungus. Hazel is especially susceptible to honey fungus when growing in the shade. This may well explain why hazel is common in regularly coppiced woods but dies out in those left uncut. In recent years the most dramatic of tree diseases is the result of a fungus spread by a beetle: Dutch elm disease, carried by the elm bark beetle, has affected the majority of elms in Essex. Essex woodland elms are famous and have been studied in great detail. Most elms sucker freely and a whole wood of elms can result from one original tree. Each wood has its own 'clone' of elms. Only the wych elm does not sucker but reproduces only by seed. This is a rare species in Essex, although in Meep's Hole, Ramsden Crays, a 0.6 hectare patch of continuous wych elm is believed to be the largest in East Anglia.

Green woodpecker at nesting hole. (RH)

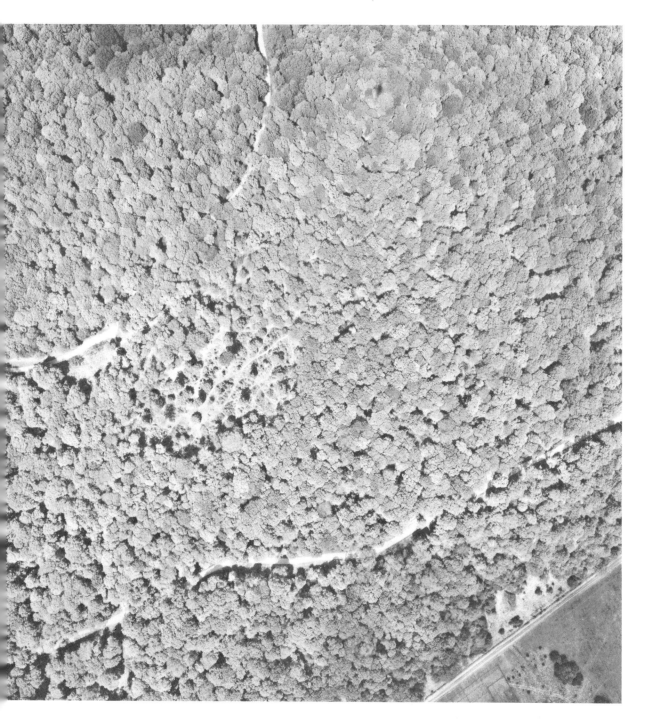

Epping Forest from the air — the dense tree cover is broken by Woodman's Glade where the trees have been experimentally re-pollarded. (UCCFAP)

ABOVE: Sunlight filters through the trees in Epping Forest. (Photo by Harold Jackson; courtesy of EFCC) LEFT: A dead oak pollard in Epping Forest: overtopped by faster growing trees. (DC) RIGHT: Special rides are maintained for horses in Epping Forest. (DC)

ABOVE: Pollarded trees on Staples Hill, Epping Forest in 1877, before the commoners lost their traditional wood-cutting rights. (EFCC) BELOW: Spotted orchids are abundant in the wide grassy rides in Bendysh Wood. (DC)

OPPOSITE ABOVE: Medieval wood-pasture with pollarded hornbeams: a traditional pattern of woodland management maintained in the National Trust's Hatfield Forest. (TI) BELOW: A massive beech pollard in Epping Forest; it has not been re-pollarded for over 100 years. Meanwhile, silver birch has colonised a once open heathy area in which the beech stood. (TI) ABOVE: A freshly coppiced clearing in Shadwell Wood: the light encourages bluebells to flower profusely. (DC) BELOW: Dormice are found in several woodland nature reserves, LEFT: in hibernation, RIGHT: newly wakened in spring. (DC)

ABOVE LEFT: Red deer have recolonised Essex and now breed in Forestry Commission woods near Saffron Walden. (DC) RIGHT: A great spotted woodpecker starting work on its nesting hole in a dead tree. (HMcS) BELOW LEFT: Toads are mainly woodland animals. (DH) RIGHT: The goldcrest breeds mainly in coniferous woodlands and is also seen on the coast during migration. (RG)

ABOVE LEFT: Ringlets are most common along sunny rides in woodland plantations. (EB) CENTRE: The small pearl-bordered fritillary was the first of the woodland fritillaries to become extinct in Essex. (DC) RIGHT: Purple hairstreaks live in many Essex woods. (DC) BELOW LEFT: The white admiral survives in a few woods in NE Essex. (DC) RIGHT: The giant woodwasp has become commoner as a result of coniferization of some woods. (DC)

LEFT: The birds' nest orchid flowers in the darkest part of a wood. (DC)
ABOVE: The presence of herb paris is a good indicator of an ancient
woodland. (MG) BELOW: Spurge laurel in Moat Wood nature reserve. (DC)
OPPOSITE ABOVE: Hornbeam fruits, with their characteristic winged
bracts, make the identification of this tree easy. (DC) LEFT: Hazel catkins
are an early spring feature of coppice woods and old hedgerows. (DC)
CENTRE: Lily-of-the-valley in flower in one of the nature reserve
woodlands in the Danbury area. (MG) RIGHT: Bluebells carpet several of
the ENT nature reserve woodlands. (DC)

78

79

79

LEFT: Wood anemones in Hockley Woods. (RG)
RIGHT: Greater butterfly orchid — a woodland
species. (EB) BELOW: The foul smell of a stinkhorn
fungus attracts flies to disperse its spores. (DC)

Rape and Burning

Harvest mice and post-harvest spraying. (JF)

In May the oilseed rape bursts into bloom and turns an area almost equal to all the county's woods a brilliant mustard yellow. Ten times this area will be green with wheat and barley until it ripens for the harvest in late July, now a couple of months ahead of the traditional harvest festival. Most of the cereals are grown by specialist farmers with no use for straw. Much straw will be burnt, leaving fields black, awaiting the autumn spray of total killer herbicide, to prepare the ground for the plough and the planting of winter cereals.

'Rape and Burning' would have been almost unheard of events on Essex farmland only 25 years ago: the area of rape planted has increased 130 times since then, and straw was more likely to be used to bed the county's cattle — then twice as numerous. The tables of statistics that follow, all taken from official Ministry of Agriculture sources, give a clear indication of the rapid changes that have occurred on Essex farms since 1959. I have chosen 1959 for the simple reason that it was the year in which the Essex Naturalists' Trust was founded: so these are the changes that conservationists have seen and commented on as they have striven to protect the county that they love. Remember that 1959 was not in the 'golden age' of nursery-book peasant farmers and abundant wildlife. The war had necessitated ploughing up much previously unproductive land and the persistent organochlorine insecticides, like DDT, were in full use.

Numbers and Areas of Essex Farms

Size (ha)	area of land (ha x 100)		Number of farms	
	1959	1981	1959	1981
200+	647	1337	219	389
40-200	1781	1144	1918	1144
20-40	235	124	814	430
<20	213	97	5805	1777
Totals	2876	2702	8756	3740

Since 1959 the area of farmland has decreased by 17,400 hectares. Most of this has gone to housing, factory building and roads — although some has gone to provide public recreation land, reservoirs and gravel-pits. In fact the total loss of farmland will be a little higher than the table indicates, because new land has been added to the farmland total by the grubbing out of woods and inning of saltmarshes, but this gain is a tiny amount compared with the loss to urban development.

Despite the loss of over 6% of its area in 25 years, farmland still covers almost 70% of the county. The shape of the landscape and the fate of most wildlife is in the hands of the 1,500 people who own and manage 90% of all the farmland in Essex. This concentration of the majority of the countryside in the hands of a comparatively few wealthy farmers has happened in the last 25 years, as small farmers have sold out to the large and successful cereal farmers.

Areas of crops and numbers of animals

Crop	1959	1982	Livestock	1959	1982
	Area (ha x 100)			numbers in hundreds	
Wheat	493	1138	Dairy cows	370	174
Barley	601	532	Other cattle	941	615
Oats	104	19	Sheep	902	620
Rape	1	132	Pigs	1778	2067
Root crops	210	105	Poultry	33137	40579
Peas and beans	73	71			
Fruit and veg.	144	45			
Fodder crops	39	86			
lying fallow	142	22			
Grass	1047	488			
(inc. rough grazing)					
Other crops	22	10			
Total croplands and grazing	2876	2648			

All the changes recorded in the tables are a result of the changing economic climate, which has always been the deciding factor in shaping agriculture. Because Essex farmland is of such high quality, farmers are free to switch their farming to whatever is the most profitable crop of the monent. The grazing animals, and the fields in which they grazed, have declined dramatically with the switch to wheat farming. The only animals that have increased are the pigs and poultry that live in factory farms and help consume the surplus grain. The decline in oat production marks the final switch from horse to tractor power.

The Ministry of Agriculture puts land into five grades. Grade 1 can grow anything, but is rare. It covers 2.3% of Essex and includes the brickearths of the Southend district (used for vegetables and early potatoes), the loams of south-west Essex used for market gardening, and the deep sandy loams of the fruit-growing area to the north-east of Colchester. Grade 2 covers nearly half of Essex (48.5%). It can be used for root crops, seed growing and fruit but most is used for cereals. Grade 3 covers most of the rest of Essex (44.1%) and is a rather variable category. It is often used for grass growing but most of it can be, and has been, persuaded to grow cereals. This 'persuasion' involves massive investment and only occurs due to the present huge subsidies on cereal production. Many of the lost flower meadows are grade 3 land that has been ploughed up. Grade 4 covers only 5.1% of the county and cannot be used for cereals because it is poorly drained. It is in this category that the few remaining damp, flower-rich meadows occur. Grade 5 is rough moorland-type land and is not found in Essex. On the basis of the proportion of the county in grades 1 and 2, Essex is the second best agricultural county in Britain (with Cambridgeshire a clear winner).

Farmland has been the dominant habitat in Essex for almost two thousand years. It is only quite recently that a combination of archaeological digs and historical researches has shown that iron age Essex was already intensively farmed and that during the Roman occupation about 50% of the county was farmland. In fact, during Roman times, cereal production was great enough for an export trade to develop. Grain was dried in efficient, heated grain driers before winter storage or export.

Most of Essex has, or had until the recent phase of field enlargement, an ancient landscape consisting of irregularly shaped fields bounded by hedges of quite exceptional antiquity. Generally these small 'do-it-yourself' shaped fields existed by the 14th century. Some of the hedgerows are considerably older than this and were probably created by leaving strips of the original wildwood rather than deliberately planting a hedge.

Neolithic and bronze age folk cut the first clearings in the wildwood and cultivated round the irremovable stumps, with simple wooden ploughs. Iron age fields had straighter sides and were ploughed with ox-drawn metal ploughs: but still half a hectare was the normal field size. It is likely, though unproven, that these iron age settlements have a continuity of farming use, through Roman to Anglo-Saxon and the present time. The landlords have changed, but the management stayed much the same. Certainly the parish and hundred boundaries, whose precise positions remain known today and which often form the present parish boundaries, are marked by the oldest and most diverse hedgerows and the lines of Roman roads.

In Roman times, fields were increased in size and, towards the end of the occupation, the introduction of the mould-board plough encouraged the cultivation of fields in long strips: the fore-runner of the standard Anglo-Saxon practice.

In two parts of Essex a more regular landscape of near equal-sized fields, hedges that run straight for long distances, and straight roads, are present-day indications of a countryside deliberately replanned by the Romans. Dengie peninsula and the Thurrock area contain the best examples of this type of landscape. These regions have few traces of Roman villas and were probably farmed as Imperial estates. Near the coast they were also centres of salt-making. Brine was boiled in clay pots to produce dry salt. Each salt factory is marked by a present day 'Red Hill' formed by the slow accumulation of charcoal and broken brine pots, creating a mound of reddish soil.

Saxon farmers used common arable fields ploughed in strips. Often the field boundary is marked by a present-day road or green lane that evolved from the track beside the field. Often, too, a steep slope marks the boundary or roadside. This is a lynchet formed by soil-creep during centuries of ploughing and rainfall on a sloping field. These open fields were subdivided into individually owned and hedged fields before 1600 over most of Essex. The 'parliamentary enclosures', where Acts of Parliament allowed enclosure of the common fields in the 18th or 19th century, were unnecessary in most of Essex: enclosure had happened by agreement centuries before. Only 2.2% of Essex was enclosed under Act of Parliament, in contrast to some parts of the East Midlands where nearly half the county was so enclosed. That is the difference between 'ancient' and 'planned' countryside.

The removal of hedgerows by farmers in arable areas is one of the commonest causes of complaint by country-lovers. It is a change that happened first, and most dramatically, in the planned countryside of the East Midlands. Hedgerow removal in Essex has not produced quite such massive prairies as are typical of much of the cereal belt — but fields have been considerably enlarged. Curiously, since Essex hedgerows are so ancient and so important, the rate of loss does not seem to have been recorded. The County Council's own Countryside Conservation Plan scarcely even mentions hedgerows in its analysis of the important Essex wildlife habitats — although an earlier publication on Historic Features in the Essex Landscape said the Council would grant-aid the replanting and restoration of ancient hedges.

An Essex Field Club survey in NW Essex found that about one third of all hedges had been removed between the war and the early 1970s. My own quick survey of part of my own parish (Wimbish) in 1983 showed that enough hedges had been removed to reduce the number of fields by half since the war. Many of the remaining hedges marked farm and parish boundaries or bordered rights of way and were the most ancient of all the hedges.

When hedges had to keep stock in the field, they would have been maintained by laying — a skilled and time-consuming task, which seems not to have been widely practised in Essex. Now hedges only function to mark boundaries, provide a bit of game-cover and maintain landscape amenity, they are maintained by cheaper means. One of the best compromises between economic farming and hedgerow wildlife conservation is to manage the hedge like a coppice wood. Cutting the hedge to ground level every ten years or so, leaving standard trees to grow on or repollarding the ancient pollards that provide the nest-sites for owls, is a system used on a number of Essex farms. The only problem is that the initial coppicing looks like hedgerow removal, and the conservationist farmer may get protests from the very country lovers he is helping.

The more usual form of management is to trim the hedge — or to flail it with a bush-whacker attachment to a tractor. In winter, when the hedge has just been flailed, it looks a terrible mess. Carelessly done, many of the hedgerow trees and shrubs fail to recover from their injuries and a thin and gappy hedge results. Flailing is so cheap and easy that it does encourage farmers to keep their hedges, rather than root them out: but it produces a hedge of much reduced value to wildlife. The main problem is that the flailing is done so frequently, whereas a coppiced hedge has years to recover between each coppicing. There seems no economic reason to flail hedges so frequently and a good deal of evidence to suggest that, in the mid-winter lull of the grain farming year, flailing a hedge is a convenient way of giving a temporarily surplus farmworker something to do.

It is often claimed that the age (in centuries) of a hedge can be estimated by counting the number of tree and shrub species in a 30 metre length. This method does not give a precise age but can distinguish new from old hedges. A pure hawthorn hedge is quite recently planted and a hedge with 12 species is certainly medieval and may go back to Roman times or beyond.

Until recently the majestic elms in most Essex hedgerows gave a special character to the rural landscape. Now Dutch elm disease has killed nearly all the mature trees, although the roots have not died and new suckers are springing up. It seems likely that our descendants will once again have mature elms in their hedges — but we will not see them in our time. Meanwhile the other hedgerow trees take on an increasing importance.

Ash and oak are present in most hedges and are now the most important 'landscape trees'. Unfortunately, both seem to be suffering from the effects of modern field drainage lowering the water-table. Ash die-back and large oaks becoming stags-heads are both associated with lack of water. The oaks in the middle of ploughed fields, left-overs from when the field was a pasture, also seem to have a higher mortality rate than woodland trees. A comparison of recent aerial photographs with 18th century estate surveys has shown that farmland trees have decreased from 10-25 trees per hectare to 10-25 per hundred hectares. In parts of south Essex, the rate of loss is even greater than one hundredfold. This rate of loss has probably now been reversed, and many farmers are careful to allow selected natural saplings in the hedges to grow on and become mature trees. In many areas these saplings are tagged with a plastic marker to remind the tractor drivers to leave them unflailed.

One of the major objections to straw-burning is the accidental damage caused to so many hedges. Although a burnt hedge will regrow, given time, burning is often a prelude to 'tidying-up' and removing the damaged hedge. The Essex Naturalists' Trust is campaigning for a total ban on straw burning: meanwhile it remains to be seen whether the strict new by-laws will prevent further damage to the remaining hedges.

Birds of farmland can be grouped depending on whether they both nest and feed in field or hedgerow, or are farmland feeders that nest elsewhere. The Common Birds Census is a national study organised by the British Trust for Ornithology to estimate the numbers of common breeding birds in farm and woodland habitats. The Essex results, based on five farmland and six woodland survey areas between 1969 and 1980, are as follows:

Average number of breeding pairs per 100 hectares of common Essex farm birds.

Species	Farmland	Woodland
Blackbird	43	100
Skylark	33	—
Dunnock	27	82
Song Thrush	18	48
Yellowhammer	18	—
Chaffinch	15	68
Wren	14	110
Robin	14	120
Greenfinch	14	33
Blue Tit	13	96
Linnet	13	—

These are the 'top-11' song birds of Essex farmlands — and the only ones to breed at average densities of above one pair to ten hectares. It is important to note that of this top 11 only the skylark is not a hedge nester — emphasising that most farm birds were woodland species originally, and will decrease on farms where hedgerows are removed. Yellowhammers and linnets nest in woodland edge and scrub, but not in full woodland included in the CBC survey. The other species are much commoner in woodland than in farmland — but, since there is eighteen times more farmland than woodland, the great majority of these birds nest in farmland. That is the real importance of farmland habitats — bringing a diversity of common species to all parts of the county rather than being a refuge for rare specialists.

These average figures hide considerable variations from place to place and year to year. Yellowhammers declined considerably during the early 1960s as a result of poisonous seed-dressings, but have now recovered their numbers. Bullfinches, not common enough to feature in the table, having an average density of only two pairs per 100 hectares, get so common near fruit growing areas that they are considered an orchard pest. Some 750 bullfinches a year were killed on one 100 hectare orchard without noticeably reducing the population.

The skylark is the only bird in the list to have increased as a result of increased cereal growing. Its density does not seem to be affected by increasing field size, and in real prairie-sized fields it will be the only breeding song bird present. The rich arable land created from coastal marshes seems especially favoured by larks; here their density can be more than double the average figure. Where the farmer specialises in growing early cash crops, such as lettuces, skylarks have caused havoc by pecking the seedlings and young plants.

It is rare for skylarks to cause such problems, and the only birds that are in the bad books of every Essex farmer are pigeons — especially woodpigeons. Woodpigeons are woodland nesters but field feeders. In winter the resident population is augmented by birds from northern Britain and, probably, from across the North Sea. Winter feeding flocks of 1,000 birds are common and can go to 8,000. In normal arable farmland of eastern England, the woodpigeon is not only the commonest bird but is the most important wild grazing animal. 40% of the weight of all birds on farms is woodpigeon. Rabbits, which once held top grazer place, have never fully recovered from the 1950s myxomatosis epidemics.

At one time woodpigeon control by shooting was encouraged by the Ministry of Agriculture, who issued free cartridges. This stopped when research showed that shooting did not affect the population at all — it was availability of winter food that controlled the population. Whether for sport or a wish to vent frustration, farmers continue to shoot woodpigeons by the thousand. But the high availability of good winter grazing on the wheat and rape crops means that the population has increased. One result has been a boom in the bird-scaring industry. Traditional scare-crows decorate the Essex fields but do little good. Electronic marvels of whirling arms and sirens are marketed by a Saffron Walden firm in numbers that suggest that at least the farmers believe they work. But far and away the most common form of bird scaring is the gas-gun, keeping up its ear-splitting explosions from dawn to dusk at fifteen minute intervals: one more source of conflict between the Essex farmer and his country-loving neighbour.

Woodpigeons are the commonest and largest pigeon, but all the other species are part of the grazing bird community on farmlands. It is interesting to see how the various species have undergone major changes of fortune. The domestic pigeon (rock dove) was once kept in the dove-cotes of most Essex squires, to graze on the cornfields of the tenants. Rural domestic pigeons, like squires and tenant farmers, are a thing of the past. Feral pigeons now live in the big towns. Stock doves increased in the early part of the century. Their numbers crashed during the poison seed-dressing period of the 1960s but have increased again. They are nowhere near as common as woodpigeons, being limited to their need to nest in hollow trees. In treeless parts of Essex stock doves are rare but have shown considerable adaptability, nesting in wartime artefacts on the Dengie peninsula and in rabbit holes on Foulness!

Collared doves did not start breeding in Essex until 1960 and have increased rapidly. They are now second in numbers to the woodpigeons and flocks of several hundred are not rare.

The turtle dove is a long-established species, but is only a summer visitor, so cannot take advantage of the increased food available on Essex farms in winter. It is confined to the more rural areas as a breeding species and leaves each autumn to run the gauntlet of the gun-happy French, despite which its numbers are still increasing slowly.

In every grassland community that has been studied, from high tundra to sub-tropical prairie, the bird community seems to consist of a fixed pattern of common birds: three species of different sized passerines, a wader, one or two grazers, and a couple of predators. The artificial 'grassland' communities of arable farms have developed exactly the same type of community (in addition to their woodland birds that depend on hedgerows). The Essex arable bird community is:

Passerines	Wader	Grazers	Predators
Skylark	Lapwing	Woodpigeon	Kestrel
Rook		Grey partridge	Carrion crow
Starling			

Rooks, while still a frequent sight, have declined drastically since the war. Rookeries in tall trees are easy to spot and count, so the decline has been fully documented. In 1956 there were 18,252 nests in 822 rookeries; by 1975 this was down to 9,738 nests in 482 rookeries. Since two-thirds of Essex rookeries were in tall elms, now lost to Dutch elm disease, it is tempting to blame the tree disease for the loss of rooks. This would seem to be a false conclusion — the decline was under way long before elm disease became widespread. Rooks specialise in probing farmland to catch soil invertebrates — earthworms and insect larvae. Stubble fields and newly cultivated land suit them fine, but in the breeding season they need access to pasture as there are less invertebrates in the soil under cereal crops and they are more difficult to get at. It is the switch away from pasture land that has caused the rook decline. The remaining rooks are moving home from dead elms: in at least one case they have set up a rookery on an electricity pylon.

Starlings breed in tree-holes or buildings and their abundance is due entirely to their specialisation in farmland habitats. Outside the breeding season they roam widely and are partial migrants. In winter, flocks gather to form huge night-time roosts — single roosts are estimated to contain a million starlings in Braxted Park and two million in Wrabness.

In winter, large populations of lapwings gather on ploughed fields all over the county. The breeding population is now much lower than before the coastal marshes were ploughed up. Although lapwings can breed on ploughed fields, in Essex this habit is largely restricted to the boulder-clay regions of the north-west. Elsewhere, lapwings breed in non-farmland habitats, such as gravel-pits and sewage farms.

The grey partridge is the true native species. For most of the year it feeds on seeds and crop plants just as avidly as a woodpigeon, although because of its sporting value farmers encourage rather than discourage it. Despite this it is declining rapidly — and as a direct result of modern farming. Grey partridges require weed seeds and insect food to breed successfully and modern sprays remove both. The decline of the native partridge is shown dramatically in the records from Essex shooting estates: 20 birds shot per 100 hectares in the 1960/61 season down to 1.5 birds twenty years later. Over the same period the number of the introduced red-legged partridge shot had increased five-fold. This is entirely due to the captive breeding and release of huge numbers of chicks. Over 10,000 red-legged partridge chicks were released on two estates in central Essex in 1981 alone.

The native grey partridge seems set for extinction unless farmers heed some recent research by the Game Conservancy. If a strip at the edge of each field is left unsprayed, the wildflowers and insects colonise the edge of the crop from the hedgerow and provide ideal partridge-breeding conditions. The lack of spraying has a negligible effect on the total cereal crop harvested and wildlife, other than the partridge, benefits as well. But, at present, almost all Essex farmers persist in spraying to the edge of their fields and beyond. Then, to complete the process, they walk round each field spraying a total killer to produce a neat brown strip of dead vegetation between the crop and the hedgerow.

Kestrels recovered quickly from the decline caused by DDT and dieldrin in the 1960s and are common; although the total population is not accurately known. The normal diet of kestrels consists of field voles. Field voles are common only in rough grassland and are almost absent from most intensively farmed habitats — which is perhaps why small birds feature to a greater extent in the diet of Essex kestrels than is normally the case. Kestrels have adapted their nesting behaviour to modern times too: taking to nest boxes at Fingringhoe Wick nature reserve and on large tracts of Ministry of Defence land and breeding on buildings or pylons in the urban fringe. But most kestrels still breed in old nests of other birds.

Although field voles are scarce on farmland, other small mammals are not. Every hedgerow has its bank voles, as does every small wood and copse. Bank voles hardly ever venture out into cultivated fields, so hedgerows must be a vital highway connecting their woodland centres of population. Wood mice, on the other hand, make a speciality of becoming field mice for part of the year. Their populations build up considerably in standing crops, especially cereal crops. After harvest, most crowd into woodland habitats, but some remain in the stubble fields and can be considerable pests where sugar beet is sown — they dig up the seeds and eat them. Yellow-necked mice are less prone to move into crop fields than are wood mice, but I have found them quite commonly moving through fields of rape on forays from their nest sites in nearby woodland. Probably their considerable climbing skills help in the jungle of a rape field.

Harvest mice, also good climbers, were once common in farm fields, and large populations would build up in stooked corn. Early harvests and combine harvesters have made fields less suitable for harvest mice — but they are still common in rough grassland and hedgerows. Whether harvest mice still use the fields in the Notley area, where long stalked cereals are grown and cut by traditional methods to supply thatching straw, has not been investigated.

The small rodents are the main prey of owls. The tawny owl, a woodland species really, is the commonest farmland owl. Barn owls, the traditional farmland species, have declined drastically and are now down to an estimated 100 pairs in the whole county. As usual, pesticides are blamed, and the slight recovery in numbers now that the most harmful pesticides have been restricted, is encouraging. It is probably loss of nest sites and the high road mortality that has prevented barn owls making more of a comeback.

Whereas the majority of farmland birds are increasing after declines due to pesticide usage twenty years ago, the decline of farm wildflowers continues and is almost complete. Two distinct types of farmland had a rich diversity of wildflowers associated with them: arable fields and hay meadows. Fields used as permanent pasture have never had a great range of wildflowers although many of the richest meadows would have been grazed for part of the year after haymaking.

Today most grass fields are 'leys' or 'improved' pasture. Leys are ploughed fields, seeded with vigorous grasses and used mainly to provide silage. 'Improving' a pasture consists of spraying with herbicide and applying fertiliser to favour grass growth at the expense of clovers and other broadleaved plants. In neither case will the field contain any wildflowers of note. The old-fashioned method of maintaining a meadow — no added fertiliser apart from dung from grazing animals or silt deposited by flooding of a riverside meadow — favours a mix of plants. Those species, like clovers, that can use symbiotic bacteria in their roots to provide their own fertilisers, will prosper. The move away from horse-drawn farm vehicles, the concentration of dairy cows on fewer farms and increased drainage allowing ploughing of previously unploughable flood-meadows, are the main factors that have resulted in the loss of most ancient meadows. The Essex Naturalists' Trust is in the middle of a survey of those few that remain. Most are tiny and often associated with small farms. It seems likely that more of these meadows will be lost, although many farmers like to have attractive meadows near the farm-house and can well afford to manage one or two fields traditionally, with lower production offset somewhat by lower input costs.

Just as woods have indicator species of wildflowers, so ancient grasslands are signed by the presence of cowslips, green-winged orchids, meadow saxifrage and yellow-rattle amongst a hundred or so other species. The lovely snakeshead fritillary once graced some Essex meadows but is now known only from a single site.

The undisturbed soil of an ancient meadow permits plants with bulbs or corms to survive, and the same lack of disturbance allows the hardworking red ants to build their hills. These ant-hills are a favourite feeding site for green woodpeckers, whose decline is also related to the loss of meadow and pasture land.

Fortunately, where an ancient meadow can be bought by a conservation body, it is fairly easy to maintain it by controlled use for hay and grazing. Hunsdon Mead is a splendid example of a meadow nature reserve beside the Stort on the borders of Essex and Hertfordshire — it is owned and managed jointly by the naturalists' trusts for the two counties. Hitchcock's Meadows in central Essex, leased by the ENT, is famous for its green-winged orchids.

Conservation of cornfield wildflowers (weeds) is a much more difficult problem. Fields bright with poppies and cornflowers are a sight no farmer would wish to see on his land. Although cornfield weeds include some of the most endangered species in Essex (and in Britain), some species manage to thrive despite the best endeavours of spray manufacturers and farmers. Black grass, wild oat and scentless mayweed are species whose tenacity, rather than beauty, can be admired in most cereal fields. On an unburnt stubble field, the exquisite flowers of scarlet pimpernel, fluellen and field pansy can still be seen until the 'Roundup' knocks them out for another year.

Although field poppies are killed by herbicides, their seeds are obviously widespread and tenacious, for any corner that the spray misses will have its crop of poppies. The same cannot be said for a majority of the wildflowers recorded by the Essex botanist Gibson as common arable weeds in the 1860s. Corncockle, corn cleavers and toothed cornsalad are just three examples of once common plants now on the verge of extinction in Britain and gone, or almost so, from Essex. The lovely field cow-wheat is down to a single Essex colony, where a few plants come up from seed each year at the edge of a cornfield.

Cornfield weed conservation would require the expensive procedure of growing arable crops whose market value would be low, for the sole benefit of the weeds. Understandably, few farmers are willing to contemplate this. One experiment, at Weeley, was tried — the field was to be a cornfield nature reserve. The agreement fell through and the Weeley cornfield is one of the very few examples of a nature reserve created by agreement with the owner, where the reserve later had to be abandoned. Although the ENT owns a small farm, the land is tenanted and conservation experiments will only really get under way when the farm comes under the complete control of the Trust.

Probably the only real hope for arable wildflowers is the 'leave the edge unsprayed and gain some partridges' idea already mentioned. This is the type of compromise between farming and wildlife, with some spinoff for sporting interests, that the Essex Farming and Wildlife Advisory Group is well placed to promote. EFWAG works by discussion and co-operation between farmers and conservation bodies like the ENT. In co-operation with the Countryside Commission, a demonstration farm and several 'farming and wildlife exercises' have been organised. The main demonstration farm, Bovingdon Hall, is farmed by John Tabor, current president of ENT. It is a good example of compromise between farming and wildlife within the existing economic environment. The latest demonstrations and experiments at Bovingdon Hall concern alternative uses for straw — in preparation for the day when straw-burning is banned.

Of course it is Government policies that have the biggest effects on the pattern of farming, and have been the cause of most of the adverse changes in the rural Essex scene in recent years. What may come as a surprise is that this has been the case for some hundreds of years. The day when Essex farms simply provided the food resources of the local community was centuries ago.

Medieval times saw the development of weaving trades to provide cloth for London and export. The demand for wool led to increased sheep keeping, the creation of sheep runs by enclosing the old common-fields and thus, in part at least, was responsible for the 'ancient' countryside features. The further development of the weaving trades in the 16th century — a result of the arrival of refugee Dutch weavers, a tax-sheltered home market and a favourable export one — created the wool towns of Braintree, Bocking, Coggeshall and several others. Sheep rearing must have become increasingly important. Weaving was the second biggest employer (after agriculture) until the trade collapsed and died in the 18th century. Essex sheep were no longer in demand but wheat certainly was.

Wheat has been a mainstay of Essex farming since Roman times. In 1700 wheat production was just high enough to feed the resident population and leave a small surplus for export to London and abroad. Essex was described as 'a level and enclosed county . . . neatly husbanded . . . enriched with all kinds of grain and stocked with great herds of kine and hogs'. London needed more grain and men of means recognised the opportunity in Essex. Farms were bought-up and improved systems of crop rotation introduced. By 1800 a traveller could write 'the great object of the Essex farmer appears to be to raise wheat; and, in our view, three-eighths of the arable land was carrying that golden crop'. About 80,000 hectares were under wheat: a figure halfway between the 1959 and 1982 areas of wheat. This amount of wheat produced three times what Essex people could eat and would have been a major 'export' crop. Profitable arable farming brought changes in land use: rabbit warrens became arable fields, woods were sold to be rooted out and make fields, and reclamation of coastal land continued apace. Sounds familiar? — this was the 18th century.

Arable farming continued to prosper until the 1870s — but through much of the 19th century it was supported by artificially high prices maintained by the corn laws. Corn laws made for rich farmers, high food prices and discontented townsfolk. Cobbett made his rural rides and campaigned for the repeal of the corn laws. The laws were repealed and cheap transport allowed imports from the vast grain belts of America and Russia. Food was cheap and Essex farmers were poor.

Much farmland was abandoned and the big houses with them. Hard working Scottish farmers moved in and made a living by chicken farming or market gardening. This situation lasted into this century: a book of coloured paintings, showing Essex to be a delightful rural backwater, was published in 1909 and the author commented 'unfriendly critics sneer that every Essex farm calls itself a hall, a fact which hints at the plain truth of this county having somewhat come down in the world'. After the period of increased food demand in the first world war, the agricultural depression continued through the 1930s.

Then the second world war, and the pressing need to maximise home food production, suddenly changed Essex farming. All possible land was ploughed and brought into production — and after the war came agricultural protectionism. First price guarantees and food subsidies, then the common agricultural policy of Europe, created the present day version of the old corn laws: a system whereby it is almost impossible for a farmer to lose money growing cereals. Farm employment has declined, farms become fewer, larger and more productive, stock farming goes as horn has given way to corn and the wildlife has disappeared from Essex farmland.

The damage done to the countryside and the worldwide economic problems associated with the present system are being recognised in high places. New Cobbetts are arising to campaign against the 20th century corn laws — and some Essex MPs are amongst them. The economics of farming in Essex is in for another major change in the not too distant future.

It is my guess that Essex farmers will not collapse into poverty and old fashioned mixed farming. If subsidies are removed, farming will change to provide for the needs of a large and comparatively well-heeled local population. Already 'pick-your-own' fruit farms and free-range chicken farms are becoming profitable close to centres of population. There is also a considerable pressure from the general public to have a chance to visit farms — evidenced by the success of access farms such as Marsh Farm at Woodham Ferrers and Hayes Hill and Holyfieldhall Farms in the Lea Valley.

Farms aimed at attracting the public to visit or buy their produce provide greater agricultural employment and more varied farm habitats. Already a large scale study aimed at investigating opportunities for increased rural employment, linked to farming and conservation and funded by the EEC, is under way in Essex. And a passable imitation of an ancient meadow can be recreated in a couple of decades — whereas to recreate an ancient woodland takes a couple of millenia. So, perhaps, the future will see farmer and nature-lover working together on the same side of the hedge, rather than arguing bitterly across the barbed wire and blackened fields.

Gulls following the plough. (RH)

ABOVE: Straw burning creates a cloud of smoke. In the distance, Essex farmland shows the typical pattern of tiny woods connected by hedgerows. (DC) LEFT: Dutch elm disease has killed most mature hedgerow elms in Essex. (DC) RIGHT: Many farmers have planted trees in field corners to compensate for lost elms and hedges. (TI)

LEFT: Field irrigation is often necessary in the dry Essex climate. Here sugar beet are watered by giant hose pipes and sprinklers. (TI) RIGHT: Big bales: a new approach to dealing with straw. (DC) BELOW: A modern arable landscape. (DC)

ABOVE: Wheat covers more than a quarter of all land in Essex. (DC) LEFT:
Weasels are widespread hunters in hedgerows. (DC) RIGHT: Skylark: one of
few bird species to breed in modern farm fields. (RG)

ABOVE: The collared dove has become a common resident during the last 25 years. (DC) BELOW: The barn owl is now a rare bird of Essex farmland. (HMcS)

ABOVE: Turtle doves are summer migrants. (HMcS) LEFT: A lapwing pulls a worm from a pasture. (RG)
RIGHT: Ghost moths (only the male is a ghostly white) are common in most areas with permanent grassland.
(DC) BELOW: White woodlice live in the nests of red ants in permanent pasture. (DC)

The chalk quarry at Grays: now an excellent nature reserve. (LW)

Chalklands and Quarries

Orchids in a chalk quarry. (JF)

Although chalk lies under all of Essex, and greatly influences the chalky boulder clay region that covers the north-western half of the county, chalk only reaches the surface in two small areas — totalling less than 3% of Essex. While small in area, the chalklands have (or had) a rich flora and fauna that is very different from the rest of the county.

The north-west Essex chalklands are part of the Chilterns, which curve up through Hertfordshire and Cambridgeshire, to peter out just inside Essex in the Strethall area. Until the 19th century these chalklands were unenclosed sheep-walks and must have resembled the rich downland habitats of southern England. The destruction of most English downland pastures has happened since the second world war — the same process happened on the Cambridge/Essex borders over 100 years ago. Babington (in his *Flora of Cambridgeshire,* published 1860) described the ploughing-up of vast acreages of species-rich chalk grassland between 1800 and 1850.

The process cannot have been quite complete, as enough downland survived to provide a habitat for a large population of chalk-hill and adonis blue butterflies, just over the border in the Royston area. Accounts of Victorian entomologists describe the beginning of the 'blue' season, when local hotels would be full of butterfly collectors. Most patrolled the downlands to spot the much prized varieties of these beautiful butterflies. The richest collectors, such as Lord Rothschild, remained in the hotels and found cheque-books more efficient than butterfly nets to capture the rarest specimens.

I must emphasise that all this happened in Cambridgeshire. The Essex downlands disappeared early and, by the time Victorian butterfly hunters were searching the area and reporting their findings in the *Victoria County History,* chalkland species were already almost extinct in our county. Adonis blues are known only from a couple of records in the Saffron Walden area in the 19th century. The same applies to the mazarine blue — a species which became extinct in the whole of Britain in the early years of this century. Chalk-hill blues also disappeared early in Essex — although they managed to breed in some non-chalk areas of the county in the middle of the 19th century. Very rare vagrants are still seen (eight in 60 years) which wander into the county from the Kent downlands or the Chilterns. The silver-spotted skipper, another nationally endangered downland butterfly, bred in Essex in both the north-west and Grays chalk areas during the last century.

When the chalk downs were enclosed and ploughed, huge fields were created — much larger than the normal Essex fields of the time. These fields have become larger still with the recent phase of hedgerow removal — but it should be remembered when looking at such areas as Strethall Field that hedgerows never were common in the area. The ancient hedgerows that are present are especially notable for the frequency with which the chalk-loving dogwood, wayfaring-tree and purging buckthorn are found. Purging buckthorn is one of the main foodplants of the brimstone butterfly, so it is not surprising that brimstones are common in the north-west part of Essex.

Strethall Field and the other large arable fields harbour many important wildflowers that are extremely rare or absent elsewhere. Three species of fumitory (small white, small pink and narrow-leaved) are known from Strethall, where they have been found with the localised round-headed and long prickly-headed poppies. The attractively named Venus's looking glass, a member of the bellflower family, is also found here. They are most common where the fields border old chalk-pits; modern herbicides seem to be causing a considerable decline in chalk arable flowers just as they have on all arable land.

The chalk fields are home to one of the rarest breeding birds in Essex: the stone-curlew. These skulking brown relatives of the plovers, with big eyes for nocturnal insect hunting, are usually associated with chalk downlands or dry, sandy, brecklands. They were known in Essex in the middle of the 19th century only from the NW chalk — where they seem to have been able to adjust to life in the middle of huge arable fields on what had once been their downland pasture.

Before the war, ornithologists had reported that stone-curlews were no longer breeding in Essex. In 1949 two breeding pairs were rediscovered at Strethall — the first reports for 47 years! A couple of years later, enquiries amongst the farmers in the region revealed that stone-curlews had been known in the area for over twenty years: a minimum of 6 pairs were breeding in Essex. It seems they had never left (at least only for their winter migrations south) — but just managed to avoid the prying binoculars of the bird-watchers. Since the rediscovery, stone-curlews are known to have bred in most years, although their range seems to be contracting towards the Cambridgeshire border and only two pairs have bred in recent years.

There must be a considerable risk that the decline in insects and seed-bearing weeds in arable fields, and the early harvests, will spell the end of the stone-curlew in Essex. It may well go the way of the corncrake — a species which no longer breeds anywhere in England. It was once widespread in Essex, but the only pairs known to have summered (and presumably bred) since the war, were at Strethall. The last was in 1955.

Between Ashdon and Bartlow, just on the Essex side of the border, are four round barrows: these are the survivors of a group of seven or eight tumuli. The largest of the Bartlow Hills rises to nearly 14 metres and has a diameter of some 45 metres. The hills are claimed to be the finest Romano-British burial mounds in Britain and clearly must be the last resting place of some once important people. Excavations carried out in the 19th century revealed cremated remains in a large square bottle, a richly enamelled vessel and many other objects judged to indicate that these are the graves of British princes buried under Roman rule but to British custom.

The Saffron Walden botanist, G.S. Gibson, must have known the Bartlow Hills well in the middle of the 19th century and recorded the rich chalk grassland flora that grew there. Pasque flowers are the most famous: Gibson reckoned them abundant in 1861, but only a single plant survived to be seen by an Essex Field Club outing in 1912. The caretaker of the hills reported that this plant survived and flowered until the 1920s. Purple-stemmed cat's-tail grass survived until 1861, field fleawort and purple milk-vetch were last seen in the 1850s. In each case these were the last records for Essex.

Early drawings of the Bartlow Hills show them as mounds rising out of treeless grassland and topped by planted tufts of trees. During this century, secondary woodland has closed around the hills and made them invisible from any distance. The hill to the north of the old railway line is itself covered in trees and ivy and is devoid of grassland flowers. The three main hills have public trackways around their bases and have been cleared of trees. Each hill is protected by a high paling fence topped by barbed wire and within this protection sycamore, elder scrub and nettles are rapidly regrowing. However, vandals have broken through the palings of two hills and, ironically, the feet of exploring trespassers are helping to restore a short-grass flora. On the top of the highest hill, beside the pit where the excavation was carried out, is chalk grassland with rockroses and wild thyme — so the hills are still harbouring flowers that have declined elsewhere in Essex.

At about the same time that British princes were being buried by the barrow load at Bartlow, other Britons were burrowing into the chalk in the south of the county. In Hangman's Wood, Grays, are the remains of over 50 deneholes. These vertical shafts go down through about 15 metres of sands and gravel to the chalk beneath. Within the chalk, chambers form a double clover-leaf pattern at the base of each shaft.

The Bartlow Hills as they were in the early 19th century, when pasque flowers grew there. (MH)

The function and origin of these deneholes has long been the subject of speculation and argument. Medieval legend had it that they were the gold-mines of King Cunobelin — the King conquered by the Romans, and the Cymbeline of Shakespeare. Serious archaeological investigations by members of the Essex Field Club late in the 19th century and again in the middle of this century suggest that medieval legend at least had the age of the deneholes right. The most generally accepted theory is that the deneholes were chalk mines — the chalk being used to lime arable fields as the Romans recorded that the British did. The alternative theory is that they served as winter stores for grain. It seems quite possible that both explanations are correct — what better use for a worked out chalk mine than to store the surplus grain produced by the agricultural innovation of liming fields?

In 1887, 51 denehole shafts were found but only 5 were open. By 1962 only a single shaft remained open. Generations of rubbish dumpers have blocked the shafts and created mounds of rubbish in the chambers. In 1962 the deneholes were found to contain three species of hibernating bats: Daubenton's, Natterer's and the brown long-eared. In the case of the Natterer's bats, the 13 individuals found in the deneholes are the only records from the county this century. There are no natural caves or modern mines in Essex and the dene-holes are one of the few hibernation sites for cave-dwelling bats in the county.

99

Hangman's Wood was declared an SSSI to protect the deneholes. It seems that little else has been done to make the protection real. Although some pot-holers still enter the deneholes, I have found no record of a visit by naturalists or archaeologists for over 20 years. That these ancient and intriguing caves have not been cleared of rubbish, explored properly and made a haven for bats by regulating human entry, is a tragedy.

The deneholes may have been ancient chalk mines, but the modern way of getting chalk, and the way used for centuries, is to dig it from quarries where the chalk is at or near the surface. In the north-west there are many old 'parish-pits' used to supply lime for arable fields. These are mostly abandoned and have become rich with flowers. A chalk-pit at Howe Wood harbours the last surviving plants of crosswort in Essex. Some of the old pits have been declared SSSIs for geological reasons (Great Chesterford pit) or included in larger SSSIs for botanical reasons (Debden Water).

Although there is a large, commercial chalk-pit near Newport Station in the north-west, the main commercial chalk quarries are in the Grays area. Chalk is mined at Grays for the cement industry and huge quarries have been created, mainly by Blue Circle Cement and its associated companies. Worked out quarries are tempting sites for disposal of rubbish or for building development, but some pits have been left long enough to become extremely rich in wildlife.

The Grays Chalk Quarry now covers about 40 hectares. Old records show that 25 hectares had been excavated by 1860 and quarrying ceased soon after the first world war. Scrub and woodland soon recolonised parts of the quarry floor and, where spring water seeps up through chalk crevices, a marshy area has formed. Among the many chalk-loving plants that colonised the quarry are 14 species of orchids — of which eight occur there regularly. This quarry is now an SSSI and is the most important site for chalk flora between the Thames and the Wash.

The twayblade is the commonest orchid, growing mainly in the wooded parts of the quarry. In dense shade the saprophytic bird's nest orchid grows. Southern marsh orchids grow with the closely related common spotted orchid and often form hybrids. In open areas and on disturbed ground the bee orchid, and its wasp orchid variety, are found. The pyramidal orchid is found mainly in the open areas at the north end of the quarry. The two real specialities of the quarry are the man orchid and the marsh helleborine — both species that are found nowhere else in Essex.

For 14 years the owners of the quarry granted the ENT a licence, renewed annually, to record the flora and undertake minor management work. The licence forbade members to enter without special permission: which meant that ENT members were just about the only people who did not have access as virtually all local people 'trespassed' freely in the quarry. Recently, and despite objections from the ENT and NCC, planning permission was given for houses to be built in the southern part of the quarry. Fortunately the granting of this permission led to Blue Circle Cement agreeing to lease the northern part of the quarry to the Trust as a full nature reserve. The 21 year lease will cost the Trust nothing, and will protect the remaining 16 hectares of quarry where the important flora are found.

The new nature reserve protects much more than the orchids. Kestrels nest on the chalk cliff. A great variety of butterflies and moths live there, including the chalk carpet — a moth found nowhere else in southern Essex. Unfortunately, the silver-studded blue, which colonised the quarry in the 1950s, did not survive the development of a more wooded environment in the 1960s. Silver-studded blues are mainly heathland butterflies, but the Grays population was of the chalkland form found mainly in Kent. Grays was the only record of this form north of the Thames.

Essex chalklands have suffered a large number of extinctions — many of which happened at the turn of the century or before. The ENT has recently bought its first small area of chalk grassland in the north of Essex: a single hectare (the Harrison Sayer reserve) protects bee orchids, fairy flax and milk vetch. Beside this nature reserve at Hadstock, on some of the highest land in Essex, stands a huge building on the edge of a wartime airfield. It is now a grain intervention store, where huge stocks of surplus grain are kept prior to their subsidised export. This summit of Essex is a peak of one of the European grain mountains. The local paper has reported hundreds of dead birds found in the area after the Ministry of Agriculture had sanctioned the laying of poisoned bait to protect the grain mountain from avian attack. The Harrison Sayer nature reserve is one of the few areas of grassland left in this part of Essex. It is to be hoped that a few more areas of chalk grassland or quarries can be preserved for their wildlife, but the real reserve for most chalkland flora will remain the roadside verges — part of the county's public and common land.

Stone-curlew at nest. (RH)

ABOVE LEFT: A bat in hibernation in a prehistoric dene-hole. (DH)
RIGHT: Brimstone butterflies are common in many parts of Essex,
including all the chalk areas of the NW. (DC) BELOW LEFT: Glow-worms
are rather rare in Essex. (DH) RIGHT: Crested cow-wheat is restricted to the
chalky regions of NW Essex. (DC)

ABOVE: Snails are most common in areas with lime or chalk rich soils. Garden snails are hermaphrodites but they still need to mate. (DC) LEFT: The rare man orchid is one of 14 species found at Grays Chalk Quarry. (DH) RIGHT: Cowslips in flower at the Harrison-Sayer nature reserve. (DC) Guelder rose CENTRE: flowers and BELOW: fruit are frequent in hedgerows and damp wood throughout Essex, but especially so in the chalk regions. (DC)

Tiptree Heath is one of the few remaining heather heaths in Essex.
(UCCFAP)

Heathlands and Commons

Common butterflies on a common. (JF)

Roadside verges are neither heathlands nor commons — but what follows is concerned with any open land that, because it is managed by a public authority or because the public has some rights over it, is neither farmed nor built on. In this sense the roadside verges of Essex are the most important of all our 'common' land. There are about 4,000 km of metalled road running through the Essex countryside, (in addition to the 3,000 km of pavement and housing edged town roads in the County Council area plus much more in the London Boroughs). Country roads all have a verge of some sort and the County Council estimates the total area of verge at 1,600 hectares. That means the average verge is two metres wide. Road verges are essentially permanent, unimproved grassland and can have a rich variety of wildflowers. The County Council's own documents, prepared in connection with the Essex Structure Plan, suggest that roadside verges are the third most important wildlife habitat in the county: coastlands and woodlands take first and second place.

There are only two species of wildflower that grow nowhere else in Britain except Essex. One is the sickle-leaved hare's-ear which was discovered as a British plant in 1832, growing on a verge at Norton Heath. It lasted 130 years on that verge. In 1962 the telegraph poles were realigned, the ditch cleared out and a bonfire built where the rarest plant in Essex had grown. Fortunately, just before the disaster, seed had been collected and the plant introduced to the ENT reserve at Fingringhoe. In 1979, sickle-leaved hare's ears reappeared on their original site — only to be sprayed out of existence in 1982 just a few months after the Government had given the plant total protection under the specially protected plants section of the Wildlife and the Countryside Act. This extreme example of accidental destruction highlights the problems associated with roadside verge conservation and management.

There are many other attractive and moderately rare roadside plants: sulphur clover, pyramidal orchid, crested cow-wheat and yellow-wort are none of them restricted to verges, but that is their main habitat. These, and many other roadside specialities, are found mainly in the chalk and chalky boulder-clay region in the Uttlesford district, where the verges have always had a greater diversity of plants.

Early in the 1970s, the Nature Conservancy Council and the ENT liaised with the Essex County Council to promote the conservation of roadside verges. An agreement was quickly reached concerning the general management of verges, which was a good compromise between the needs of road safety, economy and conservation. In addition to the general management plan, it was agreed that, where especially rich verges were identified, they could be designated as roadside nature reserves, marked with special posts and be given some extra protection from damage by digging or dumping. The survey to identify the roadside nature reserves emphasised the importance of the NW area. By 1982, 56 lengths of road had been surveyed and selected, a total of 68 km of verge. Of these, 32 lengths, totalling 50 km, were in Uttlesford.

Unfortunately, the agreement on protection of special verges has not been an unqualified success. Eight years after the Council agreed to mark the nature reserve verges, marker posts have been erected on only a tiny fraction. Some verges, containing pyramidal orchids and other rare plants, have been damaged by Council dumping of waste tarmacadam from road improvement schemes.

Traditionally, roadside verges were a source of a free hay crop for the local farmers. Now virtually all verges are cut by flail mowers and the cuttings left on the verge. This has tended to increase the soil fertility and favour the quick growing coarser plants. This is why cow parsley, hogweed and great hairy willowherb have become such a feature of Essex verges in recent years. Not only do these common species tend to out-compete the more delicate plants of low fertility verges, but the more rapid growth needs more frequent (and more expensive) cutting. The Trust is trying to encourage the Council to value its 'low fertility, low management' verges. Unfortunately, it is proving a difficult task to convince people that when a road is widened or straightened, the new verge should be left as bare soil to be colonised by wild plants and develop as a low management verge. Instead, and at considerable public expense, the new verge is covered in carefully sieved topsoil and spray seeded with grass. It then becomes a high fertility verge, costly to manage and of limited conservation value.

Far and away the most important verges are those that form an embankment beside the road. These tend to stay low in fertility and are sun-warmed with a dry soil. Rabbits help maintain a short and varied vegetation. One of my favourite verges is a steep sandy bank near Great Sampford. Common lizards, now quite a rarity in Essex, bask in the sun. Red and black burnet moths (both the six-spot and narrow-bordered five-spot species) lazily rest on the scabious flowers. Tall broomrape, a curious parasitic plant, draws its nourishment from the roots of the greater knapweed, while common blue, gatekeeper and ringlet butterflies get theirs from the flowers of the same plant. Although such verges are judged the third most important wildlife habitat in Essex, for many people they are the most important. It is the verge that everyone sees and enjoys on any walk or drive in the countryside, whereas the best woodlands and coastal areas are remote and often private.

In medieval times, roads were often much wider than today. Horse drawn traffic on muddy, unmade roads would widen the road by avoiding the worst ruts in the middle. An old statute (in 1285) required that the verges for 200 feet on either side of the road should be cleared of trees and shrubs to protect travellers from robbers. Cottagers often built their houses on the roadside waste, from late medieval times. There are many lines of cottages where the back gardens mark the original highway boundary.

Today most verge boundaries are marked by a field ditch, a hedge, or both. If there is no ditch and the hedge has been grubbed out, then farmers may steal the highway land just as cottagers did in the past. Where a ploughed field extends right to the edge of the road, it is usually possible to see a trace of the bank that marked the verge edge before the encroachment. It is a small minority of farmers that have encroached on verges and it is something the County Council has pledged itself to prevent — although I know of no cases where a farmer has been forced to relinquish a stolen verge.

While some verges have gone, important new ones have been created beside the major new motorways and trunk roads that have been built during the past twenty-five years. True motorways have reached Essex only during the last ten years and have much larger embankment and cutting verges than normal roads. When first opened, a motorway often provides a fine sight as field poppies grow in profusion on the central reservation. As the vegetation develops, the annual weeds decline and a permanent verge community develops. Already the clumps of red campions and drifts of ox-eye daisies beside the M11 make a fine contrast with the uniformity of the farm fields outside the motorway fence.

To the NE of Chelmsford, miles of the central reservation of the A12 trunk road is edged, in spring, by Danish scurvy-grass. This flower occurs naturally as a coastal, salt-loving species. Presumably the traffic from the coast has carried seeds inland and the salting of the road in winter makes the central reservation an imitation coast.

New motorway verges are not only artificially seeded, but extensive tree planting is carried out. The usual policy, on County Council roads, is to encourage planting of native tree species. The same is supposed to apply to Department of the Environment controlled motorways but large quantities of scots pine have been planted: native to Britain but hardly a typical Essex tree.

Small mammals appreciate the cover provided by roadside vegetation. Field voles are especially common amongst the long grasses beside the motorways — and it is for them that the familiar motorway kestrels are watching as they hover beside the road.

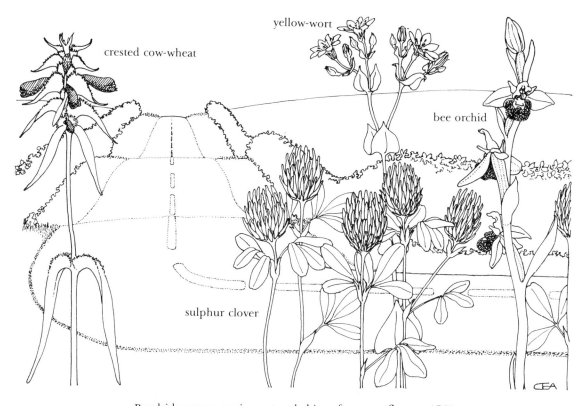

Roadside verges are important habitats for many flowers. (CA)

Every one of the nine species of small mammals in Essex (mice, voles and shrews) have been found on verges. For some, the field and bank voles, the common and pigmy shrews, verges are a major habitat. Others, like the water shrew, disperse along the verges and hedgerows to reach new ponds and streams. Apart from the hunting kestrels, a major danger to roadside mammals comes from dumped litter. They explore bottles and ring-pull cans, get trapped inside and quickly die. Naturalists have collected the remains of 'bottled mammals' to study the distribution and relative abundance of the different species. A milk bottle from Bradwell holds the world record — it contained the bones of 28 individual small mammals. Over 1,000 trapped mammals have been found in a day of searching. It seems likely that at least 100,000 shrews and voles die in discarded bottles beside Essex roads every year.

It is only during this century that most roads have been metalled — and a surprising number of unmade roads (green lanes) survive. In 1979 a Countryside Commission-sponsored study showed that Essex had 800 km of green lanes — more than any other English county except Dorset. These lanes, apart from their amenity value for walkers and horse-riders, have a great conservation value. The lanes are long strips of unimproved, flower-rich grasslands, and are usually bordered by the very oldest of hedges. Unfortunately, many of these ancient lanes have been destroyed in recent years. As long as they are classified as highways, they remain public property and are safeguarded — but they are open to any traffic that cares to drive along them and are the responsibility of the highway authority. This has tempted the County Council to reclassify some of them as bridleways — preventing motorcycle riders using the lanes but allowing farmers to plough them up. As soon as one section of a green lane has been destroyed, replaced with an unmarked right of way across a ploughed field, the remaining parts of the lane cease to be used and soon develop into thick shrub. This has certainly not happened to all the green lanes — in the north of the county many splendid examples remain, especially where they also act as farm tracks or roads to remote cottages.

Apart from green lanes, there are 6,400 km of footpaths and bridleways. Part of this massive heritage has been included within designated long-distance paths. The Essex Way leads from Epping Forest to Dedham Vale and Harwich, the Forest Way connects Hatfield and Epping Forests, while the Three Forests Way does the same by way of Hainault Forest. St Peter's Way leads from Ongar to the ancient St Peter's chapel on the coast at Bradwell. Some lengths of these ways go along green lanes and the increased use helps protect them. But although there are guide books available for the paths, proper way-marking has not been carried out along most of their length. Unless the County Council protects and way-marks the major green-lanes, bridleways and footpaths, it will have permitted a major loss of habitat to the farming interest — by default.

Railways, like roads, have verges and over 500 km of Essex railway lines provide important wildlife habitats. Because they are less disturbed by the public, railway embankments are more likely to provide homes for the larger animals. Foxes and badgers breed in holes in railway banks in several parts of the county and railways form a protected wildlife pathway along which animals can penetrate deep into the cities.

In addition to 500 km of used railway there is about 150 km of disused track. These are old branch lines in the more remote and attractive parts of the county. Rather like green lanes, abandoned railways rapidly develop into thick belts of scrub unless they are actively used or managed. One of the best uses is to create a footpath along the old track — the well marked track being easy to follow and leading the walker beside embankments of wildflowers, shrubs and butterfly-rich cuttings. The nature walkway along the old line from Bishop's Stortford to Braintree is a County Council success story. Two sections of the old Maldon-Woodham Ferrers line, at Stow Maries and Maldon Wick, have been protected as nature reserves by the ENT.

Heathland and commons have a history that is intertwined. It was the use of land as common that created the heaths. Lowland heaths, dominated by heathers, gorse or bracken, develop on free-draining acid soils used for grazing. The alkaline boulder clay has never had any heathland. Essex heaths are associated with the gravel and sandy soils which cap the ridges in southern and eastern Essex in such places as Epping Forest, Mill Green, Danbury and Tiptree. These heaths were never anywhere near as large as the huge brecklands in other parts of East Anglia — but they were a good deal more extensive than they are now.

Two factors have contributed to the loss of Essex heathlands — the natural tendency for the land to grow up into scrub and woodland if left unmanaged, and conversion to farmland after the common rights have been lost.

Tiptree Heath, although only 25 hectares in extent, is certainly the finest heath in the county. It is the only heath to have all three heather species: ling, bell heather and cross-leaved heath. The present day heath is registered common land, and an SSSI, managed by a group of volunteers under the auspices of the parish and district councils. The group's management of the heath earned it top prize in a County Council sponsored competition.

In the 16th century, Tiptree Heath covered a huge area of Danbury/Tiptree ridge. Even the remaining 25 hectares were ploughed during the second world war and have reverted to heathland since then. The reason behind the successful conservation of the heath is a policy of scrub clearance and flailing. Flail mowing promotes the development of heathers whereas, if scrub develops, either it goes on to become woodland or fires eliminate the heather and favour gorse.

Similar management is helping to maintain and extend the heather areas on the National Trust's Danbury Common, including the Backwarden area which is managed by the ENT. This common is the Essex headquarters of the rosy marbled moth — a localised species whose habitats are characterised by the presence of bracken. The caterpillar feeds on yellow tormentil.

The heathland of Epping Forest has been extensively invaded by birch scrub and heathers are becoming a rarity. Even the extensive bracken plains are shrinking — although the open grassy plains of Wanstead Flats, in the south of the Forest, are developing into broom and gorse-dominated heath.

Heathlands are the main inland habitats for the sun-loving common lizards, slow-worms and adders — all species that have declined where heathland has become closed scrub, as at Mill Green, where it is now quite difficult to find a viper near the public house of that name.

Heathland birds are mostly the familiar species of scrubland and hedgerow. Two species especially associated with heathland, the nightjar and the red-backed shrike, have both declined nationally as well as locally, and it is difficult to know whether the decline should be blamed on loss of our heathland or a more general climatic change. The 40-45 pairs of red-backed shrikes, that bred in Essex during the early 1950s, were down to a single pair by 1981. The nightjar was down from 20-25 pairs in the 1950s to none by the end of the 1960s. Since then, a few pairs have started nesting again, not on heathland, but in a young conifer plantation.

For many heathland species, the nightjar being one example, the required habitat is one with the vegetation structure of a heathland: it does not have to be a heather dominated heath. For these species a young plantation or scrub beginning to develop on waste land is a good imitation of a heath. The switch of stonechats from heathland to Thameside waste lands has already been mentioned.

Grayling butterflies require dry heathland type habitats and were once fairly widespread in the Colchester area, and also on stabilised shingle at Colne Point. They became common at Fingringhoe Wick soon after gravel digging ceased. They have now completely died out at Fingringhoe and at Colne Point, presumably not as a result of habitat changes, since the disappearance coincided with a decline over a very wide area. It was thought they had quite disappeared from Essex, but a small colony has been rediscovered on Ministry of Defence heathland just south of Colchester.

Common lands over all of England were recorded and published in 1963 as part of the Royal Commission's enquiry. This led to the Commons Registration Act under which common land now has some legal protection. In 1963, the Essex total was 68 commons and 69 village greens, covering a total of 3,465 hectares. All but 1,020 ha was Epping Forest. Most of the commons in the 20-50 ha range are heathland commons and still survive as such. These have all come under some form of public ownership or control, except Mill Green Common, owned by the lord of the manor and the largest surviving private common. 'Private common' may sound like a contradiction, but it is not. All land is owned by someone — even a common. A common is simply land on which some people other than the owner have rights to do certain things — like graze animals or cut wood.

Most of the small Essex commons, around 1-5 ha, are in a slightly different legal category. They have no known owner and are put in the care of a 'pursuant' — often the parish council. The commons may be used as recreation grounds or amenity land of some sort. There is scope for some to become important grassland nature reserves and at Ellis Green, Wimbish, the local ENT group is helping manage the common as such a reserve.

The 1960s survey also listed some large, wet grazing commons in the south of the county: Orset Fen, Bulphan Fen and Tilbury Commons covered 220 ha. In his report on the nation's commons, the late Dudley Stamp commented on these areas: '. . . low-lying areas . . . so ill-drained as to constitute fen or marsh of little value or interest'. He recommended they be drained and ploughed. The late Dudley Stamp was recognised as one of the leading nature conservationists of his day. He got his way, private acts of parliament removed the common land protection and the fens are now arable land 'of little interest', but of great value to their owners.

In many rural parishes, the small areas of common are a major part of the remaining unploughed, flower-rich grassland in the area. The other major reserve of such grassland is 'God's acre' — the parish churchyard. The County Council estimates that there are over 600 ha of churchyard in Essex — which puts it high on the list of important wildlife habitats.

Apart from the value of the undisturbed grassland, churchyards usually boast some fine mature trees and a moist environment with plenty of flying insects. This is why swallows and bats hunt around churchyards so much more frequently than over the insect-lacking arable countryside, and why few churchyards are without a pair of spotted flycatchers. The church itself often provides a safe nest site for the swallows in the shelter of the porch. The bats (mainly pipistrelles and brown long-eared) live in most Essex churches — and although they sometimes upset the churchwardens by scattering droppings in the church, they do no harm to the church fabric. Churches are home to a major part of the declining bat population — and fortunately the bats now enjoy a legal, as well as a moral, right to dwell in the house of God.

The churchyard gravestones are one of the few places where rock-loving lichens can grow. The lichens in turn are food for certain specialist moth caterpillars. It seemed most fitting that one of the leading Essex naturalists (Maitland Emmet, an expert on the smaller moths) should have discovered a colony of the lichen-feeding *Luffia ferchaultella* (a bag-worm moth) on a gravestone in Black Notley churchyard. The stone marks the last resting place of John Ray — one of the most famous early naturalists. I am sure he would have been pleased.

Nightjars. (RH)

110

LEFT: Roadside verges beside an attractive byway in central Essex. (TI)
RIGHT: Hornbeams line a hedgebank beside an ancient trackway (green
lane) at South Weald. (TI) BELOW: Lingwood Common, a birch and
bracken covered area of heathland. (RG)

ABOVE LEFT: Old gravestones provide a good habitat for lichens. (DC) RIGHT: A special post marks the start of a 'nature reserve' section of roadside verge. (DC) CENTRE LEFT: Close-mown village greens can produce an interesting crop of 'fairy rings'. (DC) RIGHT: The adder lives on dry heathy areas and is also fairly common on seawalls. (DC) BELOW LEFT: Grayling butterflies have declined and are now found in only one area of Essex. (EB) RIGHT: The grizzled skipper is now rather a rarity. (EB)

LEFT: Green-winged orchids at Hitchcocks Meadows Nature Reserve. (MG) RIGHT: Bee orchids are present on several roadside verge nature reserves. (DC) BELOW: Scarlet pimpernels bloom briefly on stubble fields after harvest. (MG)

PLATE V

Gravel pits have become important havens for aquatic wildlife: LEFT: the common blue damselfly (MG) and RIGHT: the blue-tailed damsel fly (MG) at Stanford Warren Nature Reserve. BELOW: A pair of snipe at Heybridge gravel pit. (RG)

PLATE VI

ABOVE: The emperor moth, the only British member of the silkmoth family, and its handsome caterpillar are found in many parts of Essex, including most of the heathy areas. (DC) LEFT: Common blue butterflies are found in most areas of rough grassland, including wide roadside verges. (DC) RIGHT: Common clubmoss is a rarity in Essex: it is found only at Fingringhoe Wick nature reserve. (DH)

113

LEFT: Tall broomrape on a roadside verge at Great Sampford. (DC)
ABOVE: Sulphur clover grows mainly on roadside verges in the boulder
clay region. (MG) BELOW: *Polytrichum* moss at Fingringhoe Wick nature
reserve. (DC)

Rivers and Reservoirs

Dragonfly and canal. (JF)

Essex has no natural lakes. All the large stretches of still fresh-water have been created during the last 100 years as reservoirs. Although of such recent origin, the wildlife interest of these reservoirs is considerable, the two largest being sufficiently important to have been designated SSSIs, although neither even existed before the second world war. Despite being artificial and recent, a higher proportion of the area of Essex fresh-water habitats has been given SSSI designation than any other major inland environment.

The table gives the sizes and dates of creation for the main Essex reservoirs:

Name	Size (ha)	Date flooded
Walthamstow Group (12 reservoirs)	195	late 19th century
King George V	130	1912
Abberton	500	1940
William Girling	135	1951
Hanningfield Water	350	1954
Ardleigh	55	1972
Leighs Reservoirs	11	1967

These reservoirs have become important for Essex water-birds. The ornithological importance of a reservoir increases with its size, with proximity to the sea, and with the presence of islands. Not surprisingly Abberton, which is top on all three counts, is amongst the best bird-watching areas in Essex. To be strictly accurate, Abberton's present island is a raft constructed by the Essex Water Company under guidance from the Essex Bird-watching and Preservation Society. It has become one of the few nesting sites in Essex for common terns, with up to 28 pairs breeding. To some extent the raft has made up for the loss of a real island that was present in Abberton's early years: now, due to a raised water level, the island is submerged most of the time. In its heyday, this island was the only inland breeding site in Britain for little terns and saw, in 1950, the only attempt ever made by gull-billed terns to breed in Britain.

Birds normally associated with the coast that have adapted to reservoir habitats fall into three major groups. There are those which dive and feed on fish, those which roost on water and graze on waterside vegetation and those that use the reservoirs primarily as a safe haven while roosting or moulting.

Amongst the fish-eaters, cormorants have shown the most remarkable change of behaviour in adaptation to reservoir life. Cormorants normally breed on ledges of remote sea-cliffs. Not surprisingly, Essex cormorants moved from their winter quarters around our coasts, to breed in other counties — until 1981. Then nine pairs built nests in the willows at the edge of Abberton and reared 15 young. Since then they have nested every year and the colony is growing. This is the first case in Britain, since 1916, of cormorants breeding in trees.

Wildfowl are amongst the most exciting of all birds and the reservoirs attract many thousand of them each winter. On Abberton a ringing station administered by the Wildfowl Trust has ringed 72,000 duck in 32 years — an achievement that has added a great deal to knowledge of duck migration. There are also regular monthly counts of wildfowl on all the main reservoirs. The following table, compiled from the *New Guide to the Birds of Essex,* gives the average of the peak winter counts for five winters in the late 1970s. The Lea Valley records cover all the reservoirs in the Lea Valley: William Girling and King George V as well as the twelve smaller reservoirs in the Walthamstow area. Only those species of duck that are seen every year are included.

Species	Abberton	Hanningfield	Lea Valley
Mallard	4010	730	750
Wigeon	4770	210	—
Teal	2350	800	200
Tufted Duck	1100	470	1410
Pochard	1050	350	530
Shoveler	540	200	150
Goldeneye	460	50	50
Pintail	140	210	—
Gadwall	200	140	few
Goosander	44	43	53
Smew	7	1	2

Shelduck are not in the table since they hardly ever come inland in the winter. In summer, around 60 pairs breed or attempt to breed at Abberton, and about half as many at Hanningfield. Wigeon and pintail are essentially coastal species: many more are seen on the estuaries than on reservoirs and they do not venture inland to the Lea Valley. Wigeon normally graze on coastal marshes but have adjusted to reservoir life by grazing the cereal and stubble fields which adjoin the reservoirs. By contrast, mallard and tufted duck are mainly fresh-water species and are found on all the reservoirs as well as many smaller ponds and lakes. The tufted duck move to the safety of the large reservoirs for their July/August moult and, at that time, the counts are much higher than in the winter months. Many thousand mallard have been released by wildfowling clubs. Wild mallard sometimes hybridise with farmyard ducks and the motley collection of mongrel ducks on every village pond is the result.

Between one and two hundred mute swans assemble on Abberton for the summer moult but tend to avoid reservoirs at other times. Forty to eighty of the migratory Bewick's swan winter on Abberton and commute daily to their feeding grounds on the Old Hall Marshes.

Although coastal duck will use reservoirs, wading birds generally do not — for the simple reason that the hard banks of reservoirs do not provide soft mud in which they can probe for food. When water levels are low and mud exposed, some waders are attracted. Also a high proportion of the extremely rare vagrant waders reported in Essex are seen at reservoirs. For example, the American buff-breasted sandpiper has only been seen in Essex four times — all four sightings were on reservoirs. Whether 'lost' waders prefer reservoirs, or whether it is simply that reservoirs attract large flocks of expert bird-watchers, is a debatable point. Certainly there is every reason for bird-watchers to enjoy reservoirs — the water companies co-operate closely with the bird-watching societies and allow special access permits. For the less expert, the public roads around and across Abberton and Hanningfield are excellent bird-watching spots as is the public bird hide at Abberton.

The value of islands on reservoirs has already been mentioned. Unlike Abberton, Hanningfield still has a real island on which black-headed gulls and common terns breed. The oldest, and by far the most important island is that in one of the Walthamstow reservoirs. Herons colonised this island in 1914, from the island in the Wanstead Park lake. The Wanstead heronry declined to extinction over a 40 year period as herons switched to the greater privacy of the reservoir. The Walthamstow heronry grew, and now over 100 pairs of herons nest there each year — which puts it in the top five heronries in Britain. There are some six other heronries in use in other parts of Essex — but the total nests from all six is less than that at Walthamstow.

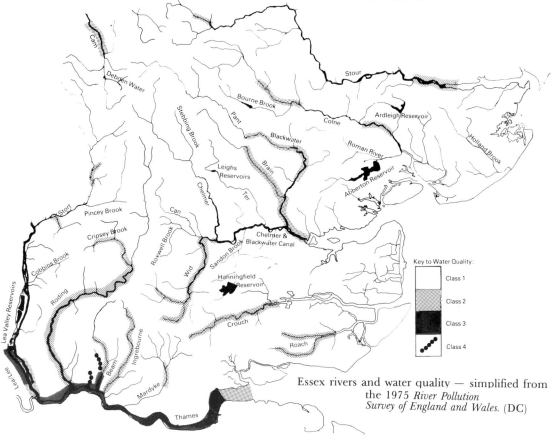

Essex rivers and water quality — simplified from the 1975 *River Pollution Survey of England and Wales.* (DC)

On the basis of the measured annual rainfall, six million tonnes of rain falls on Essex each day, on average. Put like that it sounds heavy — but in fact Essex has one of the lightest rainfalls in Britain. Much of the rain simply evaporates again or is transpired back into the atmosphere by growing plants. Some soaks down into the chalk which underlies all of Essex whence, eventually, it may be pumped out again or rise under its own pressure from an artesian well. The domestic water supply for north-west Essex is pumped from bore-holes in the chalk — which explains why the water is so hard that it can fur a kettle in a single boiling.

Only about a quarter of the rain that falls on Essex actually flows back to the sea in streams and rivers. Discounting the Thames, which is a tidal estuary along the whole of the southern border of

Essex, all Essex rivers are short, rise within the county and, with one exception, reach the sea in Essex. The one exception is the Cam which rises in the north-west of Essex and flows across the border in the one part of the county where the boundary is not itself a waterway. Obviously the boundary rivers (the Stour and the Lea/Stort) have tributaries from the counties on both sides but their Essex headwaters are in the north-west 'highlands' as are the sources of most Essex rivers.

Rivers are under the almost total control of water authorities who regulate the abstraction of water and the discharge of sewage and industrial effluent, monitor pollution levels, restock with fish and regulate angling, improve the drainage and control flooding. Essex rivers are under the control of the Thames Water Authority (TWA) if they discharge eventually into the Thames and the Anglian Water Authority (AWA) if they do not. These two authorities have been most helpful in providing a mass of statistical information used in preparing parts of this chapter.

The following table lists all the main Essex river systems — that is the rivers that reach the sea or the Thames or flow out of Essex. The many tributaries of these main rivers are not listed. To give some idea of the relative size of the rivers, the average daily flow of water is given — this is measured in cubic metres (which is the same as tonnes) of water at the measuring station closest to the mouth of each river for which statistics are available.

Thames Water Authority rivers	daily flow
Lea/Stort	449,700
Roding	224,200
Beam	35,200
Ingrebourne	33,400
Mardyke	small (not measured)
Anglian Water Authority rivers	
Cam	89,200
Stour	243,600
Holland Brook	small (not measured)
Colne	89,000
Roman River	(not measured)
Blackwater	102,800
Chelmer	88,100
Crouch	31,100
Roach	(not measured)

Most of the Dengie peninsula and the low lying land between Canvey and Grays is drained by a system of dykes and small brooks that do not join major rivers and are not included in the table.

Also omitted from the table is what could be regarded as the largest river in Essex: the northern outfall sewer which discharges over a million cubic metres a day of beautifully purified sewage into the Thames at Beckton. The return of wildlife to the Thames as a direct consequence of the purification of this sewage has already been mentioned. Nearly every Essex river has one or more discharges of treated sewage or industrial effluents running into it — indeed in many rivers treated sewage will be a major part of the flow, especially at times of low rainfall. In the Lea at Chingford about a third of the flow is sewage but the water is of adequate quality to be abstracted and, after further treatment, will supply the taps of many homes in the area. A similar story could be told of the other rivers from which water is abstracted for the domestic supply.

The water authorities categorise each section of river into one of four broad categories of water quality:

Grade 1: high amenity value and good fishing; can be abstracted for drinking after treatment.
Grade 2: moderate amenity value and coarse fishing; can be abstracted for drinking after advanced treatments.
Grade 3: fish usually absent; can be abstracted only for industrial purposes.
Grade 4: grossly polluted and likely to cause a nuisance.

The map shows that most Essex rivers are now of good quality — although there is still room for further improvement, the rivers are much less polluted than they were a few decades ago.

Although many thousands of anglers spend long hours fishing by Essex rivers, the best information on the numbers and types of fish in them comes from the water authorities who fish by less sporting methods. Recent surveys, using electric shocks to temporarily stun all the fish in a section of river, have produced much useful information. In the table, I have chosen data from three contrasting sections of river: the canalised section of the Chelmer between Chelmsford and Maldon, the mid-region of the Stour and the upper reaches of the Stour. Because fish vary tremendously in size, the total weight of fish gives a better idea of the relative importance of the species — so the table expresses the 'biomass' of each species — the weight of fish per 100 sq metres of river.

Rivers: Fish	Upper Stour	Middle Stour grams per 100 sq.m.	Chelmer Canal
Roach	334	193	199
Pike	120	172	302
Chubb	74	276	34
Dace	179	95	22
Perch	160	15	6
Eel	10	97	149
Tench	—	18	30
Bream	5	15	28
Rudd	36	—	3
Carp	11	—	4
Gudgeon	11	3	0.5
Brown trout	6	—	—
Ruffe	—	—	0.5
Stone loach	—	—	0.1

The table gives a good indication of the habitat preferences of some species: for example brown trout and dace are commoner in the smaller, better oxygenated upper Stour; while eels and pike are more common in the slow, almost lake-like, conditions of the canal. The survey did not include any small fish (below 100mm long) which explains why sticklebacks, minnows and miller's thumbs are not listed — they are quite common in most streams and rivers.

Deliberate restocking and introductions of fish for angling has had a tremendous influence on the fish stocks of Essex rivers. The AWA has recorded the introduction of a total of 175,000 fish, of seven different species, into the Chelmer and middle Stour during the six years prior to the surveys reported in the table. A hundred years ago the chubb and the brown trout were known only in the Lea — the first records of introductions to other Essex rivers were noted in the late 19th century. Although they may be of introduced origin, the fish listed in the table (with the exception of the eel) breed in the rivers and get all their food from the river ecosystem — so they are now part of the ecology of the rivers. The same cannot be said of the rainbow trout that are introduced on a 'put and take' basis in some artificial lakes and reservoirs. Captive bred fish are put in the water to be caught by anglers and taken home for the pot. The rainbow trout in these conditions are as much part of the Essex wildlife scene as a shed full of battery chickens.

One of the most unusual introductions of fish into an Essex river happened when someone emptied some surplus guppies from a tropical aquarium into the Lea. These tropical fish cannot survive in cold water but, during the 1960s, virtually all the water in the region of the Hackney power station was abstracted as cooling water and then returned to the river. At that time, most of the water was sewage, treated only to a low standard of purity, and most fish were unable to survive. In the warm and polluted water guppies bred happily — only the second known case of them breeding in the wild in Britain. Now the power station has closed down and the water is purer and cooler, the Essex guppies are extinct.

Herons fly long distances to suitable hunting grounds. Although they nest in large colonies, hunting herons work singly and can be seen standing at the water's edge on any quiet stretch of river or lake-side. Many hunt on the coastal marshes, especially in the winter. Kingfishers, too, tend to move to the lower reaches of rivers and coastal habitats in autumn and winter. They prefer slow-running, high-banked streams for breeding, the river Wid being one of the best places to see them. Numbers of kingfishers and herons are always low following a hard winter. Other factors have caused a more prolonged decline in kingfisher numbers: river dredging and 'improvement' schemes have rendered some rivers useless as breeding sites — although a couple of enterprising kingfishers have been found nesting in drain holes. Also sporadic pollution incidents, linked with fish kills and times of low rainfall, have caused declines in the south-west of Essex.

The otter was known from all the major Essex rivers in the first half of this century. It finally became extinct in the 1970s, as it did over so much of lowland England. In Essex it lingered longest on the coastal marshes and estuaries. Detailed studies on the decline of otters have put their extinction down to a combination of three main factors. First the build-up of persistent insecticides which run-off from farmland, accumulate in river fish and then get concentrated in the bodies of long-lived fish-predators like the otter. Secondly, loss of river-side breeding habitats as banks are cleared and rivers 'improved' by water authorities. Finally, human disturbance as recreational use of once quiet rivers increases, making an otter's life impossible. All three factors apply in Essex and, even though the insecticide problem is now much less severe than in the 1960s, it seems unlikely that Essex rivers will attract otters back to the county. Perhaps the feral mink which now live along several Essex rivers should be accepted as a somewhat inadequate replacement for our lost otter, although it seems a poor exchange.

Farm herbicides and fertilisers draining into streams have caused a considerable loss of water-plants. It may seem strange that fertilisers should destroy plants, but they shift the balance in favour of aquatic algae at the expense of the submerged flowering-plants that grow in clearer water. River water-crowfoot, never widespread in Essex, now seems to be restricted to a single length of the Cam near Great Chesterford. In the least polluted or 'improved' rivers, such as the Stort to the east of Harlow, a greaty variety of water weeds survive — including five species of *Potamogeton* pondweeds (curled, shining, broad-leaved, fennel and perfoliate pondweeds). Further downstream, in the Lea between Nazeing Marsh and Enfield Lock, the dominant river weed is tape grass — a semi-tropical species introduced from aquaria. The Lea is one of the few places where tape-grass grows wild in unheated water.

The nitrate and phosphate fertilisers, spread by farmers from the blue sacks which decorate our countryside, dissolve and eventually reach the rivers. The changes that these fertilisers can cause to the plant-life have already been mentioned. They can also cause problems for humans. The water authorities go to considerable expense to remove excess nitrates and phosphates from sewage before it is discharged into the rivers. It is not so easy to remove them from farm run-off. If levels get too high the river water cannot be used for drinking except after expensive treatment. In some areas of East Anglia babies have to be given bottled water as tap-water is poisonous to them, due to the high concentration of farm fertilisers. This has not yet happened in Essex, but as Essex farming uses increasing amounts of fertiliser, and that which was used years ago works its way into the water table deep in the chalk, the problems may increase.

Although the water authorities make the results of their scientific investigations freely available, even when they show that sometimes their own sewage treatment plants have failed to keep to the high standards the authorities have set themselves, there is one type of study the authorities always keep secret. These are the cost/benefit analyses which they carry out to justify the drainage and flood-prevention schemes which are enormously expensive and damaging to wildlife. It is natural for rivers to flood. The water flow in a river obviously increases greatly after heavy rainfall and the rising waters may spread out on the water-meadows beside the river. These meadows were ideal, fertile, hay meadows that can also be used for grazing in dry weather. They cannot be ploughed and do not need added fertiliser — which is provided by the flooding river. Water meadows of this type develop into some of the richest wild-flower meadows known.

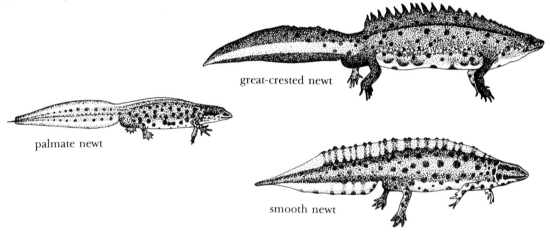

great-crested newt

palmate newt

smooth newt

All three species of newt breed in Epping Forest ponds. These are males in
the breeding season. (CA)

River improvement schemes have two main aims — to clear the river of any obstructions that might hinder rapid flow after rainfall and to reduce the risk of flooding to the riverside land to the point where draining and ploughing of the land is possible. This has two disastrous consequences for wildlife: the rich water-meadows are lost and the wildlife in the river itself is greatly reduced. It also causes other problems: drained land beside the rivers discharges rainfall into the river more quickly. The maximum flow rate may increase and can cause extra risk of flooding further downstream in towns — a risk that then needs to be avoided by more expensive flood prevention schemes. In dry weather the water that used to seep into the river from the wet meadows is not available, and the river can almost dry out apart from its constant inflow of treated sewage —which may no longer be adequately diluted.

It is easy for conservationists to think that secret cost/benefit analyses imply an unholy alliance between water authorities, drainage engineering companies and land owners, all of whom benefit from the schemes, at the expense of wildlife and the people who pay water-rates. It is usually the

Ministry of Agriculture that prevents water authorities making the cost/benefit analysis public. In 1979 the Thames Water Authority proposed a drainage scheme which would have destroyed the remaining flower rich meadows and marshes on the river Stort between Bishops Stortford and the Lea. The Nature Conservancy Council and the Essex Naturalists' Trust strongly opposed these plans and, in 1983, the water authority revised its cost/benefit analysis and deferred the plans indefinitely. This is one of the few victories of conservation over water authorities and an important one for Essex. One of the best wet meadows protected by the victory now has even greater protection: Hunsdon Mead with its masses of yellow rattle and kingcups has been bought jointly by the ENT and the Hertfordshire and Middlesex Trust for Nature Conservation. Further upstream, the same consortium owns Sawbridgeworth Marsh — the last big fresh-water marsh in the valley and one of the few places where snipe still nest.

After victory in the Stort valley the next major battle will be in the heart of Constable country. The Anglian Water Authority plans to carry out a drainage scheme in the lower Stour between Dedham and Flatford Mill.

Just as Essex lakes are actually artificial reservoirs, so the ponds are man-made too. For centuries farmers dug small ponds to act as water-holes for the cattle in their pastures. These field ponds have disappeared at an amazing rate, as farming switched to arable, or piped water was provided in the remaining pastures. The normal pattern is for a pond to be filled with farm rubbish and then covered with topsoil. These small ponds, with few if any fish in them, were the major habitat for frogs and common newts. As farm ponds have declined so garden ponds have increased. Recent surveys by the young members of the ENT have shown conclusively that garden ponds are now the main haunt of frogs in almost all of Essex.

Old village ponds remain, as do those characteristic Essex features, the moats around old and isolated farm-houses. These old moats have a wildlife community which depends entirely on the present-day management. Some moats are left shaded by a dense growth of trees — they then have no water-weeds but are excellent habitats for mosquito larvae. Others are kept open as ornamental ponds and may have a good fauna of frogs, newts, grass-snakes and dragonflies if the moat is not overstocked with ducks or goldfish.

In the 'Capability Brown' era some large landscaped parks were provided with lakes by damming small streams. At the time these were the largest fresh-water lakes in the county and acquired a rich flora and fauna. The lake in Hatfield Forest is particularly good and the marsh at its head is managed as a nature reserve by the ENT. The privately owned lake in Navestock Park has also been listed as an SSSI.

It is gravel extraction that has created the vast majority of small and medium sized bodies of still water in Essex. Since the second world war, gravel and sand digging has left huge numbers of flooded pits. These are especially abundant in the Lea valley to the north of the reservoirs, but flooded gravel pits are a feature of virtually all the former river flood-plains. It is difficult to over-emphasise the wildlife interest of these gravel pits. Little ringed plovers began nesting in 1947 and have nested annually since then — almost all nests being at gravel pits. The number of breeding great crested grebes has doubled since 1931: most nests are on gravel pits. Forty-one of the forty-eight Essex sand martin colonies are in banks excavated by gravel or sand digging.

The waste land that surrounds most flooded gravel pits is rich in insect life and offers good hunting to the adult dragonflies whose young stages live in shallow water. One of the best dragonfly habitats in the county is Fingringhoe Wick nature reserve. This complex of worked out gravel pits was bought by the ENT in 1961 and is one of three gravel pit nature reserves now owned by the Trust. So far thirteen species of dragonfly and damselfly have been identified near just one of the ponds at Fingringhoe. At Ulting, where gravel pits are close to the river Chelmer, the list of dragonflies is longer because there are some species, like the rare white-legged damselfly, that live only in unpolluted, flowing water.

Gravel digging is usually subject to strict planning control, whereas most farming operations are not. Growing demand for gravel close to London has encouraged farmers to create a large number of small irrigation reservoirs or fish ponds. These required no planning permission — and if the excavation happened to produce large quantities of gravel it could be sold off at a profit. Essex has over 200 such farm reservoirs — a British record. These unplanned 'gravel-pits' create considerable amentiy problems such as heavy traffic on small roads and unsightly developments in rural areas. Essex County Council, after many long legal wrangles, has now regained planning control over farm reservoirs. They are granted permission when there appears to be a genuine agricultural purpose for them. Whatever the amenity problems, these small reservoirs have their own wildlife value and are beginning to make up for the loss of the old fashioned farm ponds. Even small farm reservoirs attract breeding coot, little grebe, tufted duck and reed buntings.

There are ponds of many sizes in Epping Forest. The largest ones, like Connaught Water and Baldwins Hill Pond were created by damming streams. Others, like the Lost Pond, are old gravel workings. All are artificial and, like all small ponds, have a fixed lifespan. They silt up, get covered by emergent vegetation, become marshes and then dry land. To keep them as ponds requires that they be cleaned out occasionally. The Forest ponds have a particular value because they are surrounded by a large tract of woodland rather than farmland. It is for that reason that huge numbers of toads breed in the ponds: toads are woodland creatures outside the breeding season. All three newt species lives in the Forest. The rare great crested newt needs extensive hunting grounds with good ground cover near its ponds: that is why it has disappeared in farm ponds and does not easily take to ponds in small gardens. The palmate newt prefers its ponds somewhat acidic and lacking in nutrient chemicals. The forest ponds dug in the acidic gravels and free of fertiliser run-off suit it well: it is probably the commonest newt in the Forest.

Amphibians, and many of the more interesting pond insects, can only survive in ponds with limited numbers of predatory fish. This is another factor that makes the Forest ponds so important. It also means that the plan, rumoured to be under consideration, for the Thames Water Authority to carry out the much needed clearing of Forest ponds and then to stock them with fish, would spell the end for much of the aquatic wildlife in Epping Forest.

Goosander, tufted duck and smew at Abberton reservoir. (RH)

123

An aerial view of the Leighs area in central Essex. Beside the river Ter are the Leighs reservoirs and some thin strips of old pasture. Large fields indicate intensive cereal growing: the smaller speckled areas are fruit farms. The two woods on the right are nature reserves: Sandylay and Moat woods. (UCCFAP)

ABOVE: Gravel workings just to the north of Fingringhoe Wick. (DC)
BELOW: A reedbed in the gravel pit at Heybridge; Maldon in the background. (RG)

125

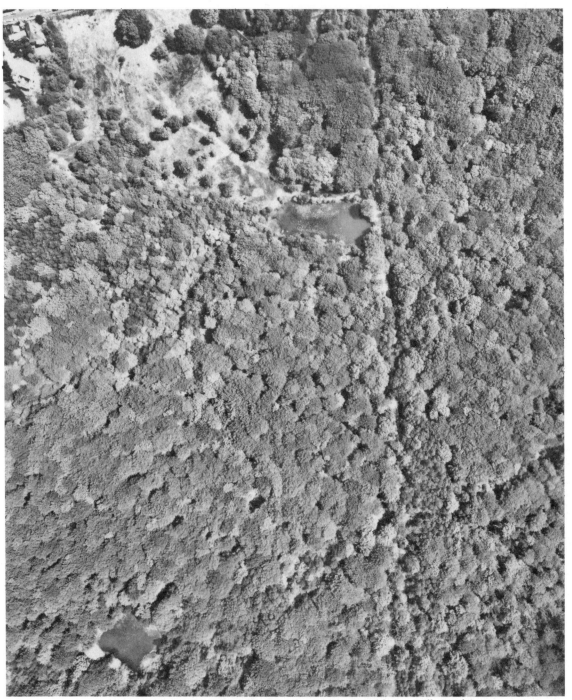

Epping Forest ponds were created in several ways. Baldwins Hill pond
(middle) was created by damming a stream. The Lost Pond (bottom of
picture) is an old gravel working. (UCCFAP) OPPOSITE LEFT: Many field
ponds have become farm rubbish dumps before being filled in completely.
(DC) RIGHT: Farmhouse moats are often the only surviving farm ponds.
(TI) BELOW: Great crested grebes breed on many Essex gravel-pits.
(HMcS)

127

ABOVE LEFT: Pike are found in all rivers and many ponds. This is a young fish from an Epping Forest pond. (DC) RIGHT: A grass-snake swimming through the water crowfoot at the edge of a small pond. (DC) CENTRE LEFT: The 'angler's curse' mayfly breeds in ponds and canals. It flies at night. (DC) RIGHT: Large mayflies *(Ephemera)* breed in fast flowing streams and fly by day. (DC) BELOW LEFT: The ruddy darter dragonfly is one of two red darters often seen near gravel-pit lakes. (EB) RIGHT: The banded demoiselle breeds in rivers. (DC)

Six examples of common Essex butterflies: ABOVE LEFT: small coppers are common on heaths and roadside verges; (DC) RIGHT: orange-tips fly in spring along country lanes; (DC) CENTRE LEFT: Essex skippers are especially common near the coast; (EB) RIGHT: speckled woods have spread widely in Essex in recent years; (EB) BELOW LEFT: gatekeepers are now the commonest butterfly along farm hedgerows, (DC) and RIGHT: peacocks are the most beautiful of the garden butterflies whose caterpillars feed on nettles. (DC)

PLATE VII

Six examples of rare Essex butterflies: ABOVE LEFT: marbled whites survive only in the Rochford area; (EB) RIGHT: green hairstreaks are restricted to heathy areas; (EB) CENTRE LEFT: the heath fritillary became extinct, but a trial re-introduction is now under way on an Essex nature reserve; (EB) RIGHT: the silver-washed fritillary is one of three large fritillaries which are now seen only as vagrants — a recolonisation may occur naturally; (EB) BELOW LEFT: white-letter hairstreaks have declined as mature elms have died (EB) and RIGHT: the purple emperor is presumed extinct in Essex, although a single specimen was seen recently in Epping Forest. (EB)

PLATE VIII

ABOVE: Broad-bodied chaser dragonflies colonise even small ponds. (DC)
CENTRE: Flowering rush (DC) and RIGHT: water-violet (MG) in flower in
Epping Forest ponds. BELOW: Pond algae can only be seen in detail with
the aid of a microscope: *Spirogyra*. (DC)

ABOVE: Abandoned 'plotlands' soon revert to woodland: part of the Basildon plotlands. (LW) LEFT: Writtle village pond — in the centre of what is now a small town. (TI) RIGHT: Garden ponds are now a major habitat for aquatic wildlife. (DC)

City and Suburbs

Town garden nightlife. (JF)

Including metropolitan Essex, built-up areas cover over 20% of the county — which makes the town environment second only to farmland in area. Despite being so different from 'natural' countryside, our towns and cities offer suitable habitats for a great variety of wildlife — with suburban gardens having a much greater diversity and abundance of bird and insect life than is usual in farmland.

What Cobbett called the 'Great Wen' of London had long been a magnet attracting the poor and unemployed from the Essex countryside to the opportunities of the city. The agricultural depression of the late nineteenth century speeded this process — and the coming of the railways caused a rapid growth of the port and seaside towns at Harwich, Clacton and Southend. The population censuses of 1871 and 1891 show that the total Essex population was increasing faster than any other county in Britain — and yet this was happening at a time when some rural areas of Uttlesford, Braintree and Dengie were undergoing a decline of population of over 30% in twenty years. The overall increase was due to populations more than doubling in east London, Tilbury, Southend, Clacton and Harwich.

A hundred years later, the 1981 census reveals a very different picture. The overall population is still increasing — but the increase is happening in the rural areas that previously showed the dramatic declines. The inner city and some large Essex towns have declining populations. Now the pattern of town growth is linked to the availability of motorways and main roads rather than railways. Beyond the greenbelt the new towns of Harlow, Basildon and South Woodham Ferrers have added large areas to the urban envionment. Almost as important are the densely built estates of 'Barrett/Wimpey/Fairview' starter homes that have been the main cause of growth in the smaller rural towns and villages.

These starter homes are the route by which so many young people can escape from the inner urban areas to an affordable home in the 'country'. A hundred years ago exactly the same dream of escape was dreamed by the dwellers in the East End — and the agricultural depression allowed the dream to become reality. The gravelly soils of the Thundersley, Basildon, Laindon and Billericay areas were rather poor agricultural land — but the new railway lines passed through them on their way to Southend. Late in the nineteenth century large areas of farmland were bought by spectators and sold off to people who wanted to build their own house, create a weekend retreat, or start a small-holding. Plots cost as little as £5 and special trains were laid on to take prospective purchasers to view them.

The sale and development of these plotlands continued into the 1930s with no planning regulations to interfere. Unmade roads and home-made homes sprawled out across the countryside. Many people gave up. Abandoned plots, whose owners had forgotten they owned them, reverted to woodland. Other, larger, ancient woods remained inside the sprawl of plotlands.

As the plotlands became a blot on the landscape they also became a haven for wildlife — especially for badgers. The dry gravelly soil would always have been good digging for badgers. The abandoned plots and woods became safe places for setts and the large gardens good foraging grounds. Many plotland dwellers are proud of, and protective towards, their badgers; and the badger's traditional enemy, the gamekeeper, disappeared when farms became plotlands. Today there are more badgers in the plotlands than anywhere else in Essex. It is an amazing experience to sit in a garden shed and watch 13 badgers playing a few feet in front of you. Even more incredible are the Laindon Hill badgers that come and knock on the door or tip over the milk bottles if their plotland protectors have forgotten to leave the usual present of food in the garden.

Foxes also prosper in plotland areas and, unlike badgers, also occur in the more densely populated parts of London. Many railway commuters have watched the fox-cubs playing outside their dens on the railway banks. In 1984 the Essex Union Hunt closed down, in effect, when it amalgamated with a neighbouring hunt — ironically its area in southern Essex has, probably, the largest fox population in the county. But because the foxes lived in urban and plotland areas they were safe from the hunters who found it increasingly difficult to get permission to hunt in the area.

Following the second world war, the unplanned plotlands were anathema to the town-planners armed with their new planning laws. Plotlands were compulsorily purchased and redeveloped as Basildon New Town and overspill estates for London. Large areas of plotland remain and a Nature Conservancy Council report has emphasised their importance for wildlife. The Basildon Development Corporation now has considerable interest in its plotland origins — some abandoned plotlands have been created as nature reserves, other parts remain as occupied plots and a 'plotland trail' runs through some of the most interesting areas.

Plotlands are notable for the large average size of gardens. But even in the more densely packed, semi-detached, metroland and modern town-planned estate, gardens occupy more land than houses and roads. Keen gardeners deliberately create a varied environment. The less keen have uniform plots of grass or more wild-looking 'natural' gardens. The overall result is a patchwork of diverse and immensely rich wildlife habitat. Anyone who has left open a brightly lit window, or placed a special moth-trap in the garden, will know that even small gardens contain literally hundreds of moth species. Many are large and beautiful like the garden tiger and the privet hawkmoth.

Birds of house and garden fall into three main groups. The summer migrants that nest in or on the house itself: swallows, house-martins and swifts are found in town and country alike. Swifts need high buildings where they can get inside the roof space and are restricted mainly to old houses and church towers. The main resident town birds that nest in or on buildings are house sparrows, starlings and feral pigeons. Sparrows and starlings are common near every building in town and country, but the feral pigeon is a specialist town dweller. Many of these pigeons are the same colour pattern as the wild rock dove from which they were domesticated, but in the urban populations the black form is most common. Black town pigeons gain the upper hand, not because of their colour, but because this variety can breed all year round — a clear advantage in towns where warmth and food are available winter and summer alike.

132

The well-loved garden birds: blackbirds, robins, blue and great tits, are really woodland and scrub species. They are much commoner in gardens than in more natural habitats because of winter food availablity. For most birds, the hard times of winter cause most deaths and set an upper limit to the population. Garden bird feeding allows birds to reach densities ten or fifteen times greater than could survive without this food. This is despite the fact that garden birds have a much higher mortality at the nestling and fledgling stage than do the country birds — but the small proportion of nestlings that survive the depredations of garden cats can expect a longer life than a country bird.

The importance of the domestic cat in the ecology of towns was underestimated until Roger Tabor's detailed study in London and Essex towns was published in 1983. Over a quarter of households surveyed had a cat — and in addition a quarter of all cats live a truly wild existence in feral colonies unattached to any one house. Feral cats have been part of the Essex scene for at least 1,500 years — although in medieval times they faced organised hunts by members of the clergy to provide the regulation cat-fur of their trade.

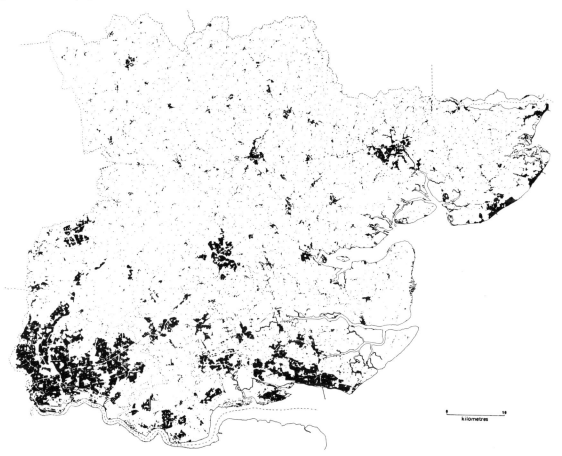

Human settlements in Essex. (Drawn by KA for *The Flora of Essex*.)

Today, the feral cats live mostly in association with factories, warehouses and hospitals: often tolerated as predators of rats and mice, fed by well-meaning employees and old ladies and then subjected to culling or sterilisation when numbers build up to nuisance levels.

The old, and now mostly derelict, warehouses along the Thames estuary would have been prime habitat for rats and cats alike. Although brown rats are all too common throughout Essex,

133

the black rat has declined dramatically since the larger brown rat spread through Britain in the 18th century. The once common black rat survived only as a ship rat and, on land, in the warehouses associated with shipping. It has disappeared from all its Essex haunts except a few warehouses in the London area — and even here it will go when the docklands are redeveloped. It seems certain that the black rat, which played such a major role in the history of Britain through its link with the plague and black death, will be the next mammal to become extinct in Essex. As yet, no-one has suggested a plan to save it from extinction.

The huge rubbish dumps, which are such a feature of Thames-side Essex, are not only good hunting grounds for brown rats and gulls of several species, in search of edible waste. These tips also attract botanists with a passion for the unusual. Many species of plant, unknown in the wild in Essex, manage to make a temporary home on rubbish dumps. Some probably arrive as waste bird-seed scraped from the budgie cage to the dust-bin. This no doubt explains the occasional cannabis plants growing illegally but unchallenged on Essex rubbish tips.

While London's solid rubbish, both from dust-bins and the huge output of fly-ash from the electricity power stations, is used to infill old gravel pits, quarries and marshes, waste gases disperse into the air. Air pollution was once a major problem — causing the infamous smogs of the 1950s. Epiphytic lichens and bryophytes are especially susceptible to air pollution and have disappeared over much of Essex. As smokeless zones and emission controls have limited air pollution, town trees are no longer soot blackened and some of the more tolerant encrusting lichens are beginning to return.

These changes have had their effects on town moth species. The evolutionary change by which the peppered moth switched from being a white and black speckled moth, camouflaged on lichen covered trees, to a black form concealed on soot covered bark, is well known. Peppered moths are common all over Essex, their stick-mimic caterpillars living on many types of roadside and garden tree. The black moth is the most common in all areas but the speckled form is still found. Interestingly, a third form may be increasing slightly — a black form with white speckling giving an overall grey appearance. This form matches rather well with the bark of most town trees which are no longer black with soot but have not been re-covered with a dense growth of lichens.

Planting trees beside urban roads has long been part of every civic authority's efforts to improve the environment. In metropolitan Essex three species were once strong favourites — presumably because they were cheap, grew well and survived the air pollution. These three are all cultivated hybrids: the common lime, hybrid black poplar and the London plane. Plane trees are unrelated to any native British tree and few species of insect live on them. By contrast, the limes and poplars are close relatives of the native small-leaved limes, aspens and sallows that were an important part of the original British wildwood. Many of the moths whose caterpillars fed on these trees have made the switch to the roadside hybrids. Poplar and lime hawkmoths, puss moths, red underwings, white satins and brindled beauties are just a few of the large and impressively beautiful moths that are quite common on roadside limes or poplars.

In recent years, road widening has eliminated many of the largest roadside trees. New plantings have tended to be of smaller, flowering trees — usually species with a limited range of associated insects. The preservation and new planting of urban limes and poplars is probably the single most important contribution that town councils could make to nature conservation. That is not to decry the efforts that many urban councils have made on behalf of wildlife. Many municipal parks now have an odd 'untidy' corner providing nest sites for birds and hibernation places for the town hedgehogs. Surveys in the Wanstead area have indicated high urban hedgehog populations.

The rate at which derelict urban ground was colonised by wildlife was first really noticed on the many bomb sites left after the last war. A previously rare bird, the black redstart, became an urban breeding species. Now the bomb sites have mostly gone, it has switched to derelict docklands, power stations and gasworks. Some councils are now using derelict land to create urban wildlife refuges — an example being the butterfly garden near Stratford station. Here wildflowers are encouraged, nettle patches cultivated to attract small tortoiseshell and peacock butterflies and a pond has been built to attract other wildlife — an imaginative scheme and a far cry from the traditional, intensively manicured town park.

Cemeteries and churchyards often provide the largest patches of open land in most urban areas. Here again there is scope for wildlife conservation — either by accident when long full sections of a cemetery are left untended, or by design for educational purposes. The best example of the latter is in East Ham, at St Mary's churchyard, where the Passmore Edwards Museum has taken over the management of a large churchyard, built an education centre, created a pond and a nature trail and preserved a rich wildlife habitat in an otherwise rather depressing part of London close to the northern outfall sewer. St Mary's is the only Essex nature reserve to have been visited by HM the Queen: she formally opened the education centre in 1983.

Poplar hawkmoths are common on roadside poplar trees in towns.
(MH)

Because of the high price of land, nature reserves are something of a rarity in most towns. No voluntary organisation can hope to buy urban land for this purpose. Most urban wildlife depends on the management of back gardens by individual residents — and it is fortunate that a majority of townsfolk have a positively welcoming attitude to wildlife in the garden. The same is not always the case with wildlife in the home. A majority of Essex bats live in occupied houses. Most are pipistrelles — far and away the commonest species — but like all bats, numbers have declined in recent decades.

Pipistrelles seem to have a positive preference for modern houses where the cavity walls, facing tiles and badly fitting barge boards provide plenty of ideal bat-nesting sites. Some bat enthusiasts have erected bat nest boxes on their houses, but it has been unkindly said that the best bat boxes are built by today's housing estate builders. Bats do no harm in houses and have full legal protection. Once householders have learnt something of their bats, and overcome any irrational fears, most are happy to share their homes with them. Helping people learn to understand and appreciate their bats is the main task of the newly formed Essex Bat Group which works in association with the Nature Conservancy Council and Essex Naturalists' Trust.

The other major task of conservation organisations in town is to help and encourage the local councils with conservation work. The London Wildlife Trust which, like the ENT, is part of the Royal Society for Nature Conservation, undertakes this task in the London area of metropolitan Essex.

Although gardens are so important for urban wildlife, it is not normally necessary or practical for a naturalists' trust to manage a garden nature reserve. A splendid exception to this rule is the ENT reserve at Warley Place near Brentwood and within a few hundred yards of the Greater London boundary. Warley Place has a distinguished history. The diarist John Evelyn lived there from 1649 to 1655 and it is said (although this is by no means certain) that it was he who introduced the early English (or purple) crocus to the gardens. Some botanists have suggested that the plant is a true native but this seems unlikely as its true home is the mountains of central and southern Europe. The real development of the gardens was due to the famous horticulturalist, Miss Ellen Wilmott, who lived at Warley Place until her death in 1934. She created crocus lawns, wild gardens and rock gardens, and introduced a host of bulbs and anemones. After her death, the house remained unused and was demolished following bomb damage in the last war. Many of the naturalised plants survived competition from wild species, as the abandoned gardens went through the usual sequence of ecological succession. When the ENT was granted a lease on the gardens it was possible to manage them in such a way that the remaining naturalised flowers continue to survive and prosper, while leaving other areas as more natural woodland with a badger sett. In spring the flowers are a superb spectacle — although the present nature reserve gardens, managed by a team of volunteers, must look very different from the time at the beginning of the century when Miss Wilmott employed over 50 full-time gardeners.

Kestrels on motorway. (RH)

Badgers live at high density in the plotland areas of south Essex. These photographs were taken at a sett in Thundersley: ABOVE: grooming; LEFT: a cub. (DH) RIGHT: A fox in full gallop escapes across a snow-covered field near the town of Brentwood. (DC)

ABOVE LEFT: Motorcars are the main predators of urban hedgehogs. (DC) RIGHT: A cock sparrow takes a drink. (RG) CENTRE LEFT: Garden ponds are one of the main breeding sites for frogs. (DC) BELOW: Yellow-tail moths are common in most gardens and woodlands. (DC) RIGHT: Peppered moths: both the original speckled form and the melanic variety; BELOW: the caterpillar is a twig mimic and lives on many town trees. (DC)

ABOVE LEFT: The strange caterpillars of the puss moth are quite common on roadside poplars in metropolitan Essex. (DC) RIGHT: Elephant hawkmoths are common amongst willow-herb on City wasteland. (DC) CENTRE LEFT: 'Woolly bear' caterpillars become RIGHT: garden tiger moths. (DC) BELOW LEFT: Sycamore moth caterpillars feed on roadside horse chestnuts as well as sycamore. (DC) RIGHT: The beautiful lime hawkmoth is common on roadside limes in town streets. (DC)

Fingringhoe Wick is the headquarters of the Essex Naturalists' Trust. The HQ buildings are visible beside the large lake — a flooded gravel pit. A varied range of habitats has been encouraged on the old gravel workings, which are surrounded by farmland and Geedons saltings beside the river Colne mudflats. (UCCFAP)

Conserving the Nature of Essex

Dormice make use of a nature reserve nest-box. (JF)

One reason why I was so pleased when Lord Buxton agreed to write the foreword to this book is that members of the Buxton family have long been a major force in the conservation of the Essex countryside. At each phase in the history of the conservation movement, there has been a Buxton involved in the work of whichever society was the most important at the time. This book has been written to mark the silver jubilee of the Essex Naturalists' Trust (ENT) and, as I hope this chapter will demonstrate, the ENT has become far and away the most important force in conserving the County's wildlife and countryside. Amongst the ENT's 60 nature reserves is one at Stansted (the Aubrey Buxton reserve) which Lord Buxton donated in 1976.

In 1852, Thomas Fowell Buxton was involved in the fight to prevent the destruction of Epping Forest by enclosure. His first court case was unsuccessful. In 1866 he tried again, this time by offering financial assistance to Tom Willingale, a Loughton commoner of the Forest, to allow him to fight for the retention of his wood-lopping rights. The case dragged on and was adjourned for ever when Tom Willingale died of old age.

In 1865 the Commons, Open Spaces and Footpaths Preservation Society was founded to do just what its lengthy name suggests. Edward North Buxton was an active local member and the society took up the cause of Epping Forest. It used its legal expertise and city contacts to persuade the Corporation of the City of London to fight a test case against all those who had enclosed Forest land. In 1874 the case was won and resulted, four years later, in the Epping Forest Act, giving the Forest into the care of the City of London Corporation to be protected for ever. E.N. Buxton was elected as one of the first verderers. It was his influence that led to the important policy decision to allow natural regeneration, rather than planting and turning the Forest into a municipal park. In effect, Epping Forest had become the first nature reserve in Essex. It is still the largest protected area in the county.

The Commons, Open Spaces and Footpaths Preservation Society (under its more manageable new name, the Open Spaces Society) still exists, although its influence in Essex has lessened. It was much involved with getting Essex common land registered in the 1960s and is now playing a major role in the 'Commons Forum' — a body that will make recommendations about future legislation that will affect all our common land.

In 1880, two years after the successful protection of the Forest, the Essex Field Club was formed. Its first title (the Epping Forest and County of Essex Naturalists' Field Club) described accurately what the club was and is: such local scientific, natural history and archaeological societies were founded in most English counties in Victorian times. E.N. Buxton was a founder member of the Essex Field Club and served on its council. In its early years, the Club was very much based in the Epping Forest area and established two local museums (the Passmore Edwards Museum in Stratford and Queen Elizabeth's Hunting Lodge at Chingford). These are now under the control of public bodies. *The Essex Naturalist,* the journal of the Essex Field Club, has provided a detailed record of natural history in the county: a record important for present-day conservation work. The Club's studies led to several early criticisms of Epping Forest management and some successful objections to unsuitable development of the Forest. Some recent publications have again voiced the Club's concern, that the present management of the Forest has paid inadequate attention to the need to maintain wildlife, by continuing the traditional pattern of forest management through pollarding and grazing.

While the Essex Field Club developed the study of natural history, the National Trust was becoming the dominant force in nature conservation. The National Trust exists solely to protect the heritage of Britain by owning and managing historic buildings and major parts of the countryside. It is the largest private land-owner in Britain. In Essex it owns 750 ha — more than half of this being Hatfield Forest.

The protection of Hatfield Forest is due, again, to the Buxton family. When, in 1923, the elderly E.N. Buxton heard that Hatfield Forest had been sold and was being felled for timber, he tried to buy it from the new owner. After some difficult negotiations he succeeded: the cheque which saved the Forest was the last he wrote. Within a few weeks of his father's death, Gerald Buxton handed the Forest over to the National Trust.

Between the wars, and as late as the 1950s, many more people were involved in the study of nature than in its conservation. The Essex Field Club had been joined by some local societies: the South Essex Natural History Society in 1934 and the Colchester and District Natural History Society in the 1950s. The Essex Bird-watching and Preservation Society, founded in 1949, soon became the largest of the county societies and publishes excellent annual bird reports. There were also a few smaller societies, and some based outside the county (notably the London Natural History Society) whose study area included part of Essex.

In 1958 the Essex Field Club was invited to send a representative to a conference concerning the development of county naturalists' trusts. Several counties had formed such trusts (the first, in Norfolk, in 1926) and the Field Club was encouraged to take the initiative in Essex. The friendly discussions with the other Essex societies were a success and the inaugural meeting was held on 2 October 1959 in Chelmsford. The first officers of the new Trust came, mostly, from the natural history societies whose work had got the Trust started. Throughout the Trust's 25 years, there have been members of its council who were also actively involved in the four major natural history societies.

Although the Essex Naturalists' Trust was founded by naturalists, its aims were the conservation of wildlife and the countryside — aims which appeal to a much wider range of people than those who join the natural history societies. None of the Essex natural history societies has ever had a membership of over a thousand — most are in the 100-400 range. Formed just as TV programmes were enthusing a wider public with an interest in wildlife conservation, the Essex Naturalists' Trust took just ten years to gain 2,000 members. Then European Conservation year really boosted interest and membership was 5,000 in 1973: it had become the largest county conservation trust in Britain — a position that it still holds at its silver jubilee with a membership of over 11,000.

The reasons for the success of the Essex Naturalists' Trust are many. Great credit must go to the energy and enthusiasm of those who are or were active council members — especially in the early years before the Trust had any paid employees to assist in its work. Within two years of its foundation, the Trust had bought its first nature reserve: a worked out gravel pit at Fingringhoe

Wick. It was great good fortune that this first reserve should have been such a mixture of varied habitats — ideal for development as an educational nature reserve and with old buildings that could eventually become a fine administrative headquarters and interpretative centre for the Trust. Fingringhoe Wick now ranks third in size of the reserves owned by the Trust — but first in its importance as a place for visitors to enjoy. A high proportion of new members have resulted from visits to Fingringhoe Wick.

The reorganisation of local government in 1974 coincided with a Trust decision to set up local groups in each of the district council areas. The idea was that, just as the Trust was involved in liaison with the County Council over planning matters, the local groups would monitor planning at the district level. As it turned out, the groups did much more than this. They became major fund-raising groups, acted as the local eyes and ears of the Trust, found many potential new nature reserves and provided social contact for the growing membership. Local groups have provided many of the volunteers that help with the management of Trust reserves and most organise programmes of lectures, rambles and film shows for members in their areas. The existence of these groups has been a third major factor in the Trust's rising membership.

At first it was feared that creating local groups would lead to competition with the independent local natural history societies. Fortunately this does not seem to have happened. Not only have the local societies retained their membership — but many new societies have been formed. By 1984 there were 19 independent societies active in Essex — in addition to 10 local groups of the ENT and many more local branches of national conservation and natural history societies. In three districts, independent local societies act as the Trust local group, and in others members of a Trust local group have formed the basis of new independent societies.

The rise of the Essex Naturalists' Trust to become the largest of all county conservation trusts, owed much to the factors chronicled above. Also, the administrative county of Essex has a higher population than any other non-metropolitan county, and so has a large potential for membership. A final factor is, perhaps, a tendency for the national conservation organisations to have been less actively involved in Essex than in other counties. The Royal Society for the Protection of Birds (RSPB) is the largest nature conservation in Europe. Its membership in Essex is probably in excess of the 11,000 members of ENT. The Chelmsford local RSPB group is foremost amongst the fund-raisers for the RSPB in Britain. And yet it was not until 1982 that the RSPB obtained its first nature reserve in Essex — at Copperas Bay. The RSPB rightly considers that a national conservation strategy for birds requires very large reserves concentrated in the most important habitats. The RSPB's recent purchase of Old Hall Marshes, part of the Blackwater Estuary national nature reserve, has established the RSPB as a major force in the conservation of Essex.

In recent years, the National Trust (NT) has tended to look away from Essex. Although the National Trust owns 750 ha of Essex compared with 630 ha owned (rather than just leased or licensed) by the Essex Naturalists' Trust, only 51 ha have been bought by the National Trust in the last 25 years. NT and ENT are often confused with each other — although they are totally separate organisations with quite different objectives. The National Trust, whilst increasingly concerned with nature conservation, is more associated with the landscape, amenity and access to the land and buildings its owns and protects. The Essex Naturalists' Trust is primarily concerned with animals, plants and wildlife habitats — whether these are to be protected by nature reserves or in the wider countryside by promoting conservation ideas amongst private landowners and public authorities.

Despite somewhat different objectives, there is a great deal of common ground between the two Trusts. Quite literally common ground — as some of the best wildlife habitats owned by the National Trust have been leased to the Essex Naturalists' Trust to be managed as nature reserves. The two large areas of access land owned by the National Trust (Hatfield Forest and Danbury/

Lingwood Commons) are managed by full-time National Trust staff and are excellent examples of how nature conservation can be integrated with fairly intensive public access and use.

Social historians have traced most of the modern conservation organisations to roots in Victorian concerns about nature, public rights and cruelty to animals. Wildlife conservation in connection with hunting goes back at least to the time of the medieval forest laws. Like most conservation organisations, the Essex Naturalists' Trust has members of opposing views concerning the ethics of hunting. As a body, the ENT tries to maintain a neutral stance about the ethics but to work with hunting organisations where this will help wildlife conservation. The most fruitful co-operation has been with with wildfowling societies. Wildfowlers have provided much useful assistance with wardening of ENT coastal nature reserves and have, at Bridgemarsh Island, bought a reserve of their own. In the campaign to protect Foulness and Maplin Sands from development, the ENT and wildfowling clubs have been united.

Shooting of pheasants and other inland birds has, through its link with intensive gamekeeping, sometimes worked to the detriment of wildlife. All the extinctions of birds of prey and predatory mammals in Victorian times can certainly be blamed on gamekeeping. Conversely, it is an interest in shooting that has persuaded a majority of Essex landowners to protect small woodlands and hedgerows on their land. In recent years, the Essex Farming and Wildlife Group, in which the ENT is represented, have used farmers' shooting interests as one prong in the campaign for improving or maintaining wildlife on farms.

Angling clubs have been at least as effective as conservation organisations in encouraging the Water Authorities to eliminate pollution and maintain good fish habitats in Essex rivers. On the other hand, the widespread introductions of fish for angling purposes and the dangers of lead weights and discarded nylon-line have harmed wildlife interests. Co-operation between angling and conservation interests has been fairly limited and could usefully be developed further.

Fox-hunting, with its needs to hunt over a wide area usually not in the ownership of the huntsmen, can cause problems in a densely populated county. Interest in fox-hunting has helped protect small woods as fox-coverts and some artificially constructed fox-earths have also benefitted badgers. Whether earth-stopping by hunts is damaging to badgers is not yet known. Hunts are not allowed to enter ENT nature reserves because of the disturbance they cause to resident wildlife — despite which there are fairly frequent complaints of unauthorised entry.

Of the many organisations that have worked with the ENT to conserve the nature of Essex, the World Wildlife Fund, in its capacity of successful fund-raiser, deserves great credit. There are several WWF supporters groups in Essex towns and grants from WWF have aided the ENT in the purchase of several of its major nature reserves.

Countryside organisations tend to fall into two broad groups — those interested in nature conservation and those concerned with public access and amenity. Partly this division reflects the occasional conflict between the two sets of objectives. More often it reflects the different origins and histories of the organisations and the fact that national government maintains the distinction with its separate Nature Conservancy Council and Countryside Commission.

Amongst the access and amenity societies, the important roles of the Open Spaces Society and the National Trust have already been mentioned. The other major societies in this group are the Essex branches of the Council for the Protection of Rural England (CPRE) and the Ramblers' Association. CPRE has developed close links with local authorities and has been especially active in conserving the town and village environments which are so much a part of rural Essex. With the Ramblers' Association, CPRE took the initiative in creating the long-distance footpaths previously described. The Ramblers' Association, as well as its work with footpaths, has helped protect Essex common land — by acting as 'pursuant' for some small commons with no known owner and also by getting some lengths of green lane designated as commons.

The Countryside Commission, the amenity side of the national government conservation effort, does not have an Essex office. Essex is regarded as part of the London and SE England region. The Countryside Commission designates national parks (of which there are none in Essex — all Britain's national parks being in upland areas) and Areas of Outstanding Natural Beauty (AONBs). The one Essex AONB is shared with Suffolk — Dedham Vale, Constable country, is what most visitors to Britain would regard as typical old English countryside. Designation as an AONB is a planning weapon that helps keep it that way. The other way in which the Countryside Commission has contributed greatly to conservation work in Essex is by directing grants towards projects that help preserve the countryside and make it accessible to everyone. The interpretative centre at the Essex Naturalists' Trust reserve at Fingringhoe, the Countryside Centre in the Dutchy Barn at Dedham and the appointment of an advisory officer by EFWAG are just three examples of the wide range of Countryside Commission grant-aided projects.

Wildlife conservation is the task of the government's Nature Conservancy Council (NCC). NCC regards Essex as part of East Anglia, it has a branch office for Essex in Colchester and the local NCC staff maintain close links with the voluntary conservation bodies — especially the ENT. The NCC has three main approaches to wildlife conservation: creating national nature reserves (NNRs), designating areas as sites of special scientific interest (SSSIs) and giving grants to help wildlife conservation.

Until recent years, the only NNR in Essex was a part of Hales Wood in the north west. Now there are large areas of coastal mudflat and some coastal marshes included within five major coastal NNRs. Colne Point, part of the Colne Estuary NNR, is fully protected because the freehold is owned by the Essex Naturalists' Trust, which receives some grant-aid from NCC to help manage this important area. For the rest of the NNRs — they are held by licence or agreement with private land-owners or local authorities. The NCC does not own any part of its national nature reserves in Essex.

Sixty-seven Essex SSSIs were designated by the NCC under the 1949 National Parks and Access to the Countryside Act. This act gave such SSSIs a planning status that meant the NCC had to be consulted before developments requiring planning permission would be allowed. It did not protect the sites against farming or forestry developments that are free from planning control. About a third of the Essex SSSIs are protected because they are nature reserves or public authority country parks of some sort. Most of the rest are in private ownership or belong to the Forestry Commission. The ENT has always regarded SSSIs as top priority when it has opportunities to buy new nature reserves.

The 1981 Wildlife and the Countryside Act was supposed to give additional protection to SSSIs as it would allow the NCC to give them some protection from damaging farming and forestry operations. The spectacular extent to which this part of the Act has failed is shown by a report published by the World Wildlife Fund and British Association of Nature Conservationists in June 1984. Designation or renotification of SSSIs under the 1981 Act requires a long process of biological survey, negotiation with land-owners and complex legal agreements. The biological resurvey work of Essex SSSIs is well advanced compared with some parts of Britain — over half have been surveyed. By July 1984 only a single privately owned SSSI has been protected by full renotification — and this despite Government assurances that renotification would be complete by the end of 1983. The NCC has been given an impossible task made doubly impossible by the Government's failure to provide it with adequate finance and staff. Essex seems to have been rather neglected, as what little man-power is available deals with the headline catching destruction of huge SSSIs elsewhere in East Anglia.

Meanwhile the NCC continues the sorry task of logging damage to the SSSIs that it has been unable to protect. Incredibly, even Epping Forest has been noted as damaged. It seems that the Corporation of the City of London, charged under one act of parliament with protecting the natural aspect of Epping Forest has, so far, failed to reach agreement on a management policy acceptable to the NCC — acting under a different act of parliament which charges it with protecting the natural environment.

Many Essex local authorities play an active part in conservation. Local authorities are empowered to buy and manage land as local nature reserves and it was the then Southend Borough Council that created the first such nature reserve in Britain when it safeguarded Belfairs Wood. The Essex new towns have also created effective local nature reserves managed mainly for their educational value. The Essex County Council and many district councils own large areas which are managed as country parks where public enjoyment of the areas is compatible with the conservation of their wildlife. Sadly, two of the district councils that look after the largest regions of Essex (Uttlesford and Braintree) have yet to create local reserves or country parks in their districts.

It is the county and district councils that play the major part in regulating the development of Essex. Essex has a good reputation for the care it takes in planning controls and shows considerable concern for countryside conservation in the Structure Plan that summarises planning policy. The planning maps have nature reserves, much wider nature conservation zones, green belts, areas of outstanding natural beauty, special landscape areas and landscape improvement areas. The village where I live is in one of the few parts of Essex that is not in one or other of these designated regions — but it seems no less attractive for that.

At the parish level there are many councils and parish protection societies that play an important role in conservation work on local commons, village greens and rights of way.

The Essex Naturalists' Trust liaises with all those organisations and councils mentioned. In its first twenty-five years it has become the most important force for the conservation of Essex wildlife and the countryside — both within the boundaries of its nature reserves and in the wider countryside. As the pressures of increasing population and farming intensification continue, the work of conserving the nature of Essex will become even more important and expensive. The Essex Naturalists' Trust is already the largest county conservation trust in Britain — but if its work is to succeed it needs more support, both from local councils and an even larger membership. Have you joined yet?

The 'scrape' at Fingringhoe Wick nature reserve. (RH)

OPPOSITE: 'I've caught a newt!' A young ENT member joins in the fun at a pond-dipping meeting. (DC)

Appendix I: Conservation land in Essex

Areas of conservation importance can be placed in three categories:

NATURE RESERVES are those areas managed by public bodies or conservation charities, where the primary management objective is nature conservation.

COUNTRY PARKS are areas managed by public bodies where nature conservation comes a close second to public access and amenity values. Not all these sites are classified as Country Parks by the Countryside Commission.

SSSIs are sites of special scientific interest designated by the Nature Conservancy Council. Many of the nature reserves and country parks are designated SSSIs and this is indicated in the lists. Many other SSSIs are privately owned or belong to public bodies such as the Forestry Commission. These are not listed as the present position is complicated by the fact that the Nature Conservancy Council is engaged in renotifying SSSIs under the new Wildlife and the Countryside Act. A full list of SSSIs notified under the old National Parks and Access to the Countryside Act can be consulted in the Countryside Conservation Plan published by Essex County Council and available in most libraries. Some of these SSSIs will be deleted or their boundaries will be changed as renotification proceeds. The NCC and ENT will publicise the new SSSIs when redesignation is completed.

SSSIs are graded: the symbol + indicates the ordinary grade which are considered of local importance. Grade 1★ are sites of international importance, grade 1 of national importance and grade 2 are of equivalent or only slightly inferior merit to those in grade 1.

All areas are given in hectares; there are about 2.5 acres in a hectare.

Key

BR	British Rail.	LNR	Local Nature Reserve.
CEC	Crown Estate Commissioners.	LVRP	Lee Valley Regional Park.
CEGB	Central Electricity Generating Board.	LWT	London Wildlife Trust.
CHA	Crouch Harbour Authority.	NCC	Nature Conservancy Council.
CL	Corporation of the City of London.	NNR	National Nature Reserve.
DC	District Council (or London Borough) of area covering the reserve.	NT	National Trust.
ECC	Essex County Council.	PC	Parish Council of relevant area.
ENT	Essex Naturalists' Trust.	PRI	Privately owned or managed.
GLC	Greater London Council.	RSPB	Royal Society for the Protection of Birds.
HMTNC	Hertfordshire and Middlesex Trust for Nature Conservation.	WT	Woodland Trust.

Access ★: access to members of owning body or to non-members by permit.

Access ★★: no access except by special permit.

Access fp: public footpaths allow the public to see part or all of the reserve.

Access pt: public nature trails with restricted opening times.

Access open: free and unrestricted entry at all times.

NATURE RESERVES

Name	Map ref	Area (ha)	owner	managed	SSSI	Access
ALDER CARR & NEWLAND GROVE	TL715113	4.5	PRI	ENT	—	★(fp)
Alder carr, grassland and woodland.						
AUBREY BUXTON RESERVE	TL521264	10	ENT	ENT	—	★
Parkland, woods and small lakes.						
BACKWARDEN	TL782039	12	NT	ENT	+	open
Part of Danbury Common, wood, heath, pools and marsh.						
BARNES SPINNEY	TM257227	0.8	ENT	ENT	—	★★
A large garden with a fine showing of both cultivated and native plants.						

Name	Grid ref	Area	Owner	Mgmt	Status	Access
BIRCH WOOD & ADJOINING WOOD	TL769068	6	ENT/PRI	ENT	+	open

Part of Danbury complex of woods, oak/hornbeam with much birch.

| BELFAIRS LNR | TQ823877 | 35 | DC | DC | + | open |

Hornbeam and chestnut coppices.

| BLACKWATER ESTUARY NNR | TL955078 | 1031 | CEC/RSPB | NCC | 1★ | ★★(fp) |

Part at TL983122. North Blackwater foreshore and the new RSPB reserve at Old Hall Marshes.

| BLAKES WOOD | TL775064 | 42 | NT | ENT | + | open |

Hornbeam and chestnut coppice, good bluebell wood.

| BONNER'S SALTINGS | TM011154 | 24 | PRI | ENT | 1★ | ★ |

Tidal saltmarsh sheltered by Mersea Island, access route to Ray Island.

| BRADWELL SHELLBANK & SALTINGS | TM035081 | 81 | PRI | ENT | 1★ | ★ |

Shell spit and saltings.

| CANVEY POINT | TQ882832 | 28 | PRI | ENT | 2 | open |

Clay, mud and shell spit with foreshore feeding grounds for wildfowl.

| CHIGBOROUGH LAKES | TL877086 | 19 | ENT/PRI | ENT | — | ★ |

Flooded gravel pits, willow grove, marsh, scrub and grassland.

| COLNE ESTUARY NNR | TM060135 | 300 | PRI/ECC/DC | NCC | 1★ | ★★ |

Other parts at TM097135 and TM076167. Tidal foreshore and beach at Mersea (open access) and grazing marsh at Brightlingsea. Also includes Colne Point qv.

| COLNE POINT | TM018125 | 277 | ENT | ENT | 1★ | ★ |

Shingle spits, saltmarsh and mudflats. Now of NNR status.

| COLNE VALLEY RESERVE | TL868292 | 2 | ECC | ENT | — | open |

Old railway embankment.

| COPPERAS BAY | TM190320 | 75 | RSPB | RSPB | 1 | ★fp |

Saltings, mudflats and adjacent fields. Major wildfowl site.

| COPPERAS WOOD | TM200315 | 14 | ENT | ENT | + | ★(fp) |

Coastal chestnut coppice and lime grove, with rare plants and moths.

| CRANHAM MARSH | TQ569854 | 13 | DC | ENT | — | ★(fp) |

Marshy fenland with three woodlands. Rich flora. Proposed new SSSI.

| DAWS HALL, LAMARSH | TL888368 | 8.1 | PRI | ENT | — | ★★ |

Marsh, woodland and pond on river bank.

| DENGIE NNR | TM045033 | 2011 | CEC/CHA | NCC | 1★ | none |

Tidal foreshore of Dengie peninsula.

| ELMS SPINNEY | TL614136 | 0.7 | PRI | ENT | — | ★ |

A field corner marsh and woodland thicket.

| FINGRINGHOE WICK | TM041195 | 51 | ENT | ENT | 1★ | pt |

Gravel pit lake, ponds, scrub and saltmarsh. Visitor centre and trails.

| GRAYS CHALK QUARRY | TQ609788 | 16 | PRI | ENT | + | ★ |

Disused quarry with rare orchids and other chalk flowers.

| GREAT HOLLAND PITS | TM205191 | 16 | ENT | ENT | — | ★ |

Ponds, stream, grazing meadow, wood and scrub on site of old gravel pits.

| HALES WOOD | TL572404 | 8.1 | PRI | NCC | 2 | ★★ |

Chalky boulder clay woodland: oxlips.

| HALL WOOD, NORTH FAMBRIDGE | TQ854987 | 3.2 | PRI | ENT | — | ★ |

Oak, ash and elm wood with rookery.

| HAMFORD WATER NNR | TM235255 | 688 | CEC | NCC | 1 | none |

Tidal flats in Hamford Water SSSI.

| HARLOW MARSH | TL452114 | 0.5 | DC | DC | + | open |

Marsh, reedswamp and alder carr with wide range of wetland flora.

| HARRISON SAYER RESERVE | TL558439 | 1 | ENT | ENT | — | ★ |

Remnant chalk grassland with rich flora.

| HATFIELD FOREST MARSH | TL539202 | 1.8 | NT | ENT | 2 | ★★ |

Base rich marsh at end of artificial lake, rich flora.

HAWKSMERE SPRING	TQ508992	1.7	ENT	ENT	—	★
Ancient, flower-rich pasture with stream and tiny wood.						
HITCHCOCK'S MEADOWS	TL788049	3.6	PRI	ENT	+	★
Unimproved, ancient pasture maintained for flowers by grazing management.						
HOGMARSH	TM102326	4.9	ENT	ENT	1	★
Saltmarsh in middle of tidal river forming boundary of Essex & Suffolk.						
HUNSDON MEAD	TL421115	28	ENT	ENT	+	★(fp)
Wet, flower-rich, meadowland between canal and river. Shared with HMTNC.						
IRON LATCH MEADOW	TL951261	2.5	BR	ENT	—	★
Ancient meadowland and some scrub.						
JOHN WESTON RESERVE	TM266245	3.6	DC	ENT	+	open
Scrub, old meadow and ponds, inside seawall. Important migrant bird habitat.						
LOSHES MEADOW	TL874369	6.9	PRI	ENT	—	★
Meadow and woodland with spring flushes and small brook.						
LEIGH NNR	TQ825855	257	DC	ENT	2	open
Part of Two-tree island plus saltings and mudflats. Brent goose feeding grounds.						
MALDON WICK	TL842057	6.5	PRI	ENT	—	open
Old rail embankment, good butterfly habitat.						
MARKS HILL & BUTLERS GROVE	TQ683874	16	DC	DC	—	open
Old plotlands with public nature trail.						
NORSEY WOOD LNR	TQ686955	69	DC	DC	+	open
Ancient chestnut coppice with standards. Good ground flora.						
NORTHEY ISLAND	TL871057	116	NT	NT	1★	★★
Saltmarsh and grazing marsh island in Blackwater estuary.						
PARDON WOOD LNR	TL447067	21	DC	DC	+	pt
Hornbeam coppice, traditional management, education centre.						
PELHAM SUB-STATION	TL458286	28	CEGB	ECC	—	★
Educational nature reserve and education centre.						
PHEASANTHOUSE FARM	TL787069	23	ENT	PRI	—	★★(fp)
Tenanted arable farm with pasture and small wood. No access normally.						
PHEASANTHOUSE WOOD	TL787065	6.5	ENT	ENT	+	open
Oak/hornbeam wood with chestnut and beech. Sphagnum bog.						
POORS PIECE	TL788068	3.2	PRI	ENT	+	open
Coppice with marshy area and badger sett.						
POPE MILL POND	TL692436	0.1	PRI	ENT	—	★
Small duck and frog pond.						
RAT ISLAND	TM055172	14	DC	ENT	1★	★★
Saltmarsh island, black-headed gull breeding colony.						
RAY ISLAND	TM005145	45	NT	ENT	1★	open
Saltings, foreshore shingle and a grass and scrub covered island.						
ROMAN RIVER VALLEY	TL974211	17	PRI	ENT	—	★
Woodland and marsh with a stream.						
SAINT MARY'S CHURCHYARD	TQ430823	3.6	DC	DC	—	pt
Urban educational reserve in East Ham churchyard. Museum centre.						
SAINT PETER'S MARSH	TL757237	0.1	ENT	ENT	—	★
Frog breeding marsh in urban environment.						
SANDYLAY & MOAT WOODS	TL738175	7.5	ENT	ENT	—	★(fp)
Coppice woods and stream. Good ground flora.						
SAWBRIDGEWORTH MARSH	TL493158	8.9	ENT	ENT	+	★
The best remaining marshland in the Stort valley. Shared with HMTNC.						
SCRUBS WOOD	TL787258	4	ENT	ENT	+	open
Coppice woodland with stream and pond.						
SHADWELL WOOD	TL573414	7.1	ENT	ENT	+	★
Ancient coppice wood, traditional management, rich flora includes oxlips.						

Name	Map ref	Area (ha)	owner	managed	SSSI	Access
SHOTGATE THICKETS	TL768941	2.2	PRI	ENT	—	★
Oak wood and blackthorn thicket beside River Crouch.						
SKIPPERS ISLAND	TM215245	94	ENT	ENT	1	★★
Island in Hamford Water including saltings.						
STANFORD WARREN	TQ686812	12	PRI	ENT	—	fp
The largest reedbed in Essex plus saltmarsh.						
STOUR WOOD	TM190315	54	WT	RSPB	+	fp
Chestnut coppice with great diversity of flora and fauna.						
STOW MARIES HALT	TQ835992	2.4	ENT/PRI	ENT	—	★(fp)
Thick hedgerows beside disused railway line and adjoining meadow.						
THRIFT WOOD, BICKNACRE	TL790015	19	PRI	ENT	—	★(fp)
Hornbeam coppice under oak standards. Wood ant nests and cow-wheat.						
THUNDERSLEY OAKS	TQ782891	0.2	ENT	ENT	—	★
Urban spinney.						
TURNER'S SPRING	TL520243	3.2	ENT	ENT	—	★(fp)
Bluebell woodland and wet meadow.						
WARLEY PLACE	TQ583908	6.1	PRI	ENT	—	★
Old gardens with many naturalized and wild plants.						
WATERHALL MEADOWS	TL759070	2.3	ENT	ENT	—	★
Wet meadow on west bank of Sandon Brook.						
WEELEYHALL WOOD	TM156212	32	ENT	ENT	+	★
Mature oak wood, with chestnut coppice and fine bluebell carpet.						
WEST WOOD, SAMPFORD	TL625332	23	ENT	ENT	+	★(fp)
Oxlip wood, with rich woodland flora, bird life and butterflies.						
WESTHOUSE WOOD	TL975272	2.8	PRI	ENT	—	★(fp)
Ancient coppiced woodland, with pond.						
WITTON WOOD SPINNEY	TM236204	<0.1	BR	ENT	—	★
Small spinney in urban setting.						
WOODHAM FEN	TQ800978	8.1	PC	ENT	—	open
Saltmarsh grading towards freshwater marsh at head of creek.						
WOODHAM WALTER COMMON	TL790065	32	PC	ENT	+	open
Oak/hornbeam wood with lily-of-the-valley. Heathland restoration attempts.						
VANGE	TQ731867	1.3	ENT	ENT	—	★★
Saltmarsh and seawall.						

COUNTRY PARKS

Name	Map ref	Area (ha)	owner	managed	SSSI	Access
BARKING MARSH – CURZON PROJECT	TQ450836	13	CEGB	LWT	—	pt
City farm and nature reserve on old ash lagoons.						
BEDFORDS PARK	TQ515923	81	DC	DC		open
Deerpark (still with red deer) and wood-pasture. Nature trails.						
BELHUS WOODS	TQ565825	38	ECC	ECC	—	open
Access woodland.						
CHALKNEY WOOD	TL873273	26	ECC	ECC	+	open
Ancient woodland with much small-leaved lime.						
CLAYTON HILL	TL390052	12	LVRP	LVRP	—	open
Hill and lake with fine views.						
CUDMORE GROVE	TM064147	14	ECC	ECC	—	open
Beach and picnic area on Mersea Island.						
CURTISMILL GREEN	TQ517965	55	DC	DC	+	open
Common land with damp woodland and some rare plants.						
DANBURY COMMON	TL782043	51	NT	NT	+	open
Heathland with gorse and scrub. Backwarden NR adjoins (q.v.).						

DANBURY PARK	TL769048	17	ECC	ECC	—	open

Old parkland, woodland and ornamental lakes.

| EPPING FOREST | TQ425995 | 2430 | CL | CL | 2 | open |

Major forest, plains and ponds. 1200 ha is SSSI woodland and considerable extension is proposed.

| GALLEYWOOD COMMON | TL725025 | 47 | DC | DC | — | open |

Relict heathland and bog plus secondary woodland.

| GARNETTS WOOD | TL635185 | 25 | ECC | ECC | + | open |

Ancient wood, well developed coppice structure.

| GRANGEWATERS/MARDYKE | TQ594804 | 51 | ECC | DC | — | open |

Hay meadows and river walk with bridleway beside wood. Continues to TQ572793.

| HADLEIGH | TQ795868 | 108 | ECC | ECC | 2 | open |

Fields and woods overlooking Thames estuary, ancient grassland and scrub with several rare plants.

| HAINAULT FOREST | TQ472933 | 385 | GLC | GLC | — | open |

Remnant of major royal forest. Similar to Epping Forest: pollards. Proposed new SSSI.

| HATFIELD FOREST | TL530200 | 421 | NT | NT | 2 | open |

The best surviving medieval, compartmented wood-pasture in Britain.

| HAVERING REGIONAL PARK | TQ500930 | 65 | GLC | GLC | — | open |

Woodland and pasture.

| HOCKLEY WOODS | TQ834923 | 120 | DC | DC | — | open |

Ancient coppice wood with traditional management being restarted.

| HYLANDS PARK | TL685840 | 178 | DC | DC | — | open |

Landscaped park with woodland and lakes. Good bird-watching.

| LANGDON HILLS EAST | TQ697861 | 55 | ECC | ECC | — | open |

One Tree Hill. Plotlands and woodlands.

| LANGDON HILLS WEST | TQ682866 | 27 | ECC | ECC | — | open |

Westley Heights, plotlands and woodlands.

| LINGWOOD COMMON | TL780060 | 20 | NT | NT | + | open |

A wooded, heathy common.

| MARSH FARM | TQ810960 | 97 | ECC | ECC | — | open |

Grazed farmland on coastal site with saltings nature reserve.

| NAZE, WALTON-ON-THE-NAZE | TM267238 | 22 | DC | DC | + | open |

Open space additional to John Weston nature reserve (qv) plus red crag cliffs.

| RAYLEIGH MOUNT | TQ805909 | 1.6 | NT | DC | — | open |

Mound which is site of Domesday castle.

| TIPTREE HEATH | TL882145 | 25 | PRI | PC | + | open |

Largest heather heath in Essex. Well managed for heathland flora.

| THORNDON PARK NORTH | TQ605915 | 84 | ECC | ECC | + | open |

Old parkland with wide range of habitats.

| THORNDON PARK SOUTH | TQ634899 | 62 | ECC | ECC | + | open |

Old parkland with wide range of habitats.

| THUNDERSLEY GT COMMON | TQ795895 | 15 | DC | DC | — | open |

Relict heathland and scrub with several rare plants.

| WALTHAM ABBEY | TQ386010 | 28 | LVRP | LVRP | — | open |

Water meadows beside Lea.

| WALTHAMSTOW MARSHES | TQ352875 | 38 | LVRP/BR | LVRP | — | ★★(fp) |

Proposed new SSSI. Important reed beds and riverside area. Part owned by British Waterways Board.

| WAT TYLER PARK | TQ744867 | 73 | DC | DC | + | open |

Coastal marsh, scrub, reed beds. Good for migrant birds.

| WEALD PARK | TQ568942 | 173 | ECC | ECC | — | open |

Ancient deerpark now managed as wood pasture and woodland. Ponds.

| WOODREDON & WARLIES | TQ424997 | 88 | GLC | GLC | — | fp |

Farm and woodland.

Appendix II: References and Further Reading

REFERENCES AND FURTHER READING: the general works which were my major sources for each chapter are listed here together with the full details of all publications referred to in the species index.

ADAMS, K. (1983). Essex Red-data Plants. Essex Field Club Bulletin 28:19-22.

ADAMS, W.M. (1984). Implementing the Act. (Wildlife & Countryside Act) WWF/BANC.

ALLEN, R. & COWLIN. R.A.D. (1971). The Badger in relation to Geology in South West Essex. Essex Naturalist 32: 307-312.

ANGLIAN WATER AUTHORITY (1978). Survey of the Fish Populations of the River Wid.

ANGLIAN WATER AUTHORITY (1978). Survey of Fish Populations of the River Colne.

ANGLIAN WATER AUTHORITY (1981). Fish populations in the Upper Stour.

ANGLIAN WATER AUTHORITY (1981). Fisheries Survey of the Chelmer and Blackwater Canal.

ANGLIAN WATER AUTHORITY (1981). Fisheries Survey of the Middle River Stour.

ANON. (no date). The Thames Estuary. WWF/NCC/RSPB.

BARNES, R.S.K. & COUGHLAN, J. (1971). A Survey of the Bottom Fauna of the Blackwater Estuary: 1970. Essex Naturalist 32: 263-276.

BASILDON DEVELOPMENT CORPORATION (1984). A Plotland Album.

BENTON, E. (1982). Dragonflies of Essex. Essex Field Club Bulletin 26: 3-8.

BOARDMAN, D.J., WILBERFORCE, P. & WARD, B.T. (1970). The Fungi of Epping Forest. Essex Naturalist 32: 277-299 & 331-340.

BOOKER, J. (1974). Essex and the Industrial Revolution. Essex County Council/ERO.

BOORMAN, L.A. & RANWELL, D.S. (1977). Ecology of Maplin Sands. Institute of Terrestrial Ecology/NERC.

BROWN, A.F.J. (1969). Essex at Work 1700-1815. Essex County Council/ERO.

BROWN, A.F.J. (1972). Essex People 1750-1900. Essex County Council/ERO.

BUCKLEY, D.G. (ed) (1980). Archaeology in Essex to AD 1500. Council for British Archaeology.

CHAPMAN, D.I. (1971). Deer of Essex. Essex Field Club.

COLCHESTER & DISTRICT NHS & FIELD CLUB: serial publication: NATURE IN NORTH-EAST ESSEX.

CORKE, D. (ed) (1978). Epping Forest: the natural aspect? Essex Field Club.

CORKE, D. (ed) (1979). The Wildlife of Epping Forest. Essex Field Club.

CORKE, D. & HARRIS, S. (1972). The Small Mammals of Essex. Essex Naturalist 33: 32-59.

COWLIN, R.A.D., (1972). The Distribution of the Badger in Essex. Essex Naturalist 31: 1-8.

COX, S. (1974). A New Guide to the Birds of Essex. Essex Bird-watching and Preservation Society.

DARTINGTON AMENITY RESEARCH TRUST (1979). Green lanes. Countryside Commission.

DAVIS, D.S. (1967). The marine Fauna of the Blackwater Estuary and Adjacent Waters, Essex. Essex Naturalist 32: 2-61.

DEPT OF THE ENVIRONMENT (1978). River Pollution Survey of England and Wales updated 1975. HMSO.

EDWARDS, A.C., (1978). A History of Essex. Phillimore.

EMMET, A.M. (1981). The Smaller Moths of Essex. Essex Field Club.

EMMET A.M. & PYMAN, G.A. (1984). The Larger Moths and Butterflies of Essex. Essex Field Club.

ESSEX BIOLOGICAL RECORDS CENTRES. (1983). A Provisional Atlas of the Amphibians and Reptiles of Essex. Passmore Edwards Museum.

ESSEX BIRD-WATCHING AND PRESERVATION SOCIETY: serial publication: ESSEX BIRD REPORT.

ESSEX COUNTY COUNCIL (1982). Essex Structure Plan.

ESSEX COUNTY COUNCIL (1981). Countryside Conservation Plan.

ESSEX FIELD CLUB: serial publications: ESSEX NATURALIST & BULLETIN OF ESSEX FIELD CLUB.

ESSEX NATURALISTS' TRUST: serial publications: BULLETIN OF THE ESSEX NATURALISTS' TRUST & WATCH OVER ESSEX.

FIRMIN. J. et al. (1975). A Guide to the Butterflies and Larger Moths of Essex. Essex Naturalists' Trust.

FORSYTH, L. (1978). Tiptree Heath. Essex Field Club.

FORSYTH, L. (1983). Fingringhoe Wick: a gravel pit nature reserve. Essex Naturalists' Trust.

GREEN, G. (1982). Epping Forest through the Ages. Published by the author.

HAMMOND, P. (1979). Beetles in Epping Forest. (in Corke (1979) qv).

HANSON, M.W. (1983). Lords Bushes. Essex Field Club.

HARRIS, S. (1972). The history and distribution of squirrels in Essex. Essex Naturalist 33: 64-78.

HUNTER, J.M. (1974). Essex Landscape No 1: Historic Features. Essex County Council.
ILLSLEY, T.W.B. & GRIFFITHS, D.T. (eds) (1976). Essex: a guide to the countryside. County Guide Publications.
JERMYN, S.T. (1974). The Flora of Essex. Essex Naturalists' Trust.
LAVER, H. (1898). The Mammals, Reptiles and Fishes of Essex. Essex Field Club.
LONDON NATURAL HISTORY SOCIETY: serial publications: LONDON NATURALIST & LONDON BIRD REPORT.
LONG, S.P. & MASON, C.F. (1983). Saltmarsh Ecology. Blackie.
MACCONNELL, J. (ed) (1977). Landscape History and Habitat Management. South Essex Natural History Society.
MILLIGAN. G.M. (1965). The Seaweeds of the Blackwater Estuary. Essex Naturalist 31: 309-327.
MONCRIEFF, A.R.H. (1909). Essex. A. & C. Black.
MURPHY, M.C. (1984). Report on Farming in the Eastern Counties of England 1982/83. University of Cambridge.
OFFICE OF POPULATION CENSUSES & SURVEYS (1984). 1981 census reports: Essex, London and historical sections. HMSO.
PEVSNER, N. (1965). The Buildings of England: Essex. Penguin.
RACKHAM, O. (1976). Trees and Woodland in the British Landscape. Dent.
RACKHAM, O. (1978). Archaeology and Landuse History: in Corke (1978) qv.
RACKHAM, O. (1980). Ancient Woodland. Arnold.
RATCLIFFE, D.A. (ed) (1977). A Nature Conservation Review. Cambridge University Press.
RUMBLE, A. (ed) (1983). Domesday Book: Essex. Original and translation. Phillimore.
SEEAR, M. (1964). Notes on the Mammals of Essex. Essex Naturalist 31: 176-187.
SKINNER, J.F. (1976). The Wildlife of South East Essex. Museums Service, Southend-on-Sea.
SMITH, J.R. (1970). Foulness. Essex County Council/ERO.
SOUTH ESSEX NHS: serial publication: SOUTH ESSEX NATURALIST.
SWALE, E.M.F. & BELCHER, J.H. (1959, 1964). The Algal Flora of the River Lee. Essex Naturalist 30: 173-178 & 31: 193-198.
THAMES WATER AUTHORITY. (no date). Fish Found in the Tidal Thames.
THAMES WATER AUTHORITY (1983). Water Statistics 1982.
WHEELER, A.C. (in preparation). Fishes of Essex. Essex Field Club.
WOOD. R.G.E. (1975). Agriculture in Essex c1840-1900. Essex County Council/ERO.

Key to Caption Credits

The following abbreviations are used in the caption credits. In all cases the artists and photographers retain the copyright of their work, which is reproduced here with their permission.

KA	Ken Adams	AH	Alan Harris
RA	Ron Allen	RH	Richard Hull
CA	Claire Appleby	DH	Don Hunford
EB	Ted Benton	SL	Stephen Long
DC	David Corke	HMcS	H. McSweeney
EFCC	Epping Forest Conservation Centre	PEM	Passmore Edwards Museum
JF	Joanna Foley	RAE	Royal Aircraft Establishment, Farnborough
TI	Terry Illsley		
RG	Bob Glover	LW	Lewis Woodward
MG	Martin Gregory	UCCFAP	University of Cambridge Committee for Aerial Photography
MH	Mark Hanson		

Index

Species

In the hope of making *Nature of Essex* pleasant reading, I have avoided scientific names in the text. For those who want to follow-up a particular point, this will be a regrettable omission which I hope this index will put right. It is intended·to serve several purposes:

SPECIES INDEX: Every species of plant or animal mentioned in the text is indexed alphabetically within the larger taxonomic groupings (Mammals, Birds etc).
SCIENTIFIC NAMES are given for each species indexed. In some cases the English name refers to a group of species within a genus, in which case the scientific name will consist of the generic name only.
MAJOR GROUPS OF ANIMALS AND PLANTS: most published studies are concerned with a single group of plants and animals. At the start of each group's section in the species index is a summary of the numbers of species known in Essex and references to the most important studies of the group in Essex.

1. MAMMALS

Of the 33 species of land mammal that have bred in Essex in historic times, 8 were introduced by man and 10 are extinct. In addition, 9 species of bat are known and several marine mammals occur in the seas around Essex. Laver (1898) and Seear (1964) give general information. Chapman (1971) on deer, Corke and Harris (1972) on small mammals, Cowlin (1972) on badgers and Harris (1974) on squirrels give more recent information on these mammals.

2. BIRDS

127 species breed in Essex (or have done so in recent years) — of these 10 are introduced. A further 105 species are regular migrants or visitors and 103, rare vagrants or visitors. At least 12 species which bred regularly at some time in the last 120 years no longer do so. The splendid new guide to the birds of Essex (Cox, 1984) gives details of all species and refers to all the earlier work on Essex birds. The annual reports of the Essex Bird-watching and Preservation Society will keep the guide up-to-date.

Species	Scientific name	Page refs.
Duck, Tufted	*Aythya fuligula*	116,123,*123*
Dunlin	*Calidris alpina*	*17,30,36,37,38, 43,45*
Dunnock	*Prunella modularis*	85
Flycatcher, Spotted	*Musicapa striata*	110
Fulmar	*Fulmarus glacialis*	48
Gadwall	*Anas strepera*	116
Godwit, Bar-tailed	*Limosa lapponica*	37,38,*43,44*
Black-tailed	*Limosa limosa*	38
Goldcrest	*Regulus regulus*	68,76
Goldeneye	*Bucephala clangula*	116
Goosander	*Mergus merganser*	116,*123*
Goose, Brent	*Branta bernicola*	*4,10,35,36,38,41, 42,50,56*
Grebe, Great Crested	*Podiceps cristatus*	122,*127*
Little	*Tachybaptus ruficollis*	123
Greenfinch	*Carduelis chloris*	85
Greenshank	*Tringa nebularia*	23,38
Gull, Black-headed	*Larus ridibundus*	24,49,90,117
Harrier, Hen	*Circus cyaneus*	55
Hawfinch	*Coccothraustes coccothraustes*	68
Heron	*Ardea cinerea*	117,120
Jackdaw	*Corvus monedula*	68
Kestrel	*Falco tinnunculus*	52,86,87,100, 107,*136*
Kingfisher	*Alcedo atthis*	120
Kite, Red	*Milvus milvus*	*18*
Knot	*Calidris canutus*	38
Lapwing	*Vanellus vanellus*	38,52,86,87,*95*
Linnet	*Carduelis cannabina*	85
Mallard	*Anas platyrhynchos*	116
Martin, House	*Delichon urbica*	132
Sand	*Riparia riparia*	48,53,122
Moorhen	*Gallinula chloropus*	52
Nightingale	*Luscinia megarhynchos*	68
Nightjar	*Caprimulgus europaeus*	109,*110*
Nuthatch	*Sitta europaea*	68
Owl, Barn	*Tyto alba*	87,*94*
Little	*Athene noctua*	68
Short-eared	*Asio flammeus*	51
Tawny	*Strix aluco*	69,87
Oystercatcher	*Haematopus ostralegus*	28,37,38,53,*53*
Partridge, Grey	*Perdix perdix*	86,87
Red-legged	*Alectoris rufa*	87
Pigeon, Feral	*Columba livia*	85,86,132
Pintail	*Anas acuta*	38,116
Pipit, Rock	*Anthus spinoletta*	23
Plover, Golden	*Pluvialis apricaria*	38
Grey	*Pluvialis squatarola*	30,38,*42*
Little Ringed	*Charadrius dubius*	122
Ringed	*Charadrius hiaticula*	25,*28,30,31*,38, 53
Pochard	*Aythya ferina*	116
Redpoll	*Carduelis flammea*	68
Redshank	*Tringa totanus*	23,37,38,*42*,opp *48*,52,57
Spotted	*Tringa erythropus*	23
Redstart	*Phoenicurus phoenicurus*	68
Black	*Phoenicurus ochruros*	134
Reedling, Bearded	*Panurus biarmicus*	52
Robin	*Erithacus rubecula*	85,133
Rook	*Corvus frugilegus*	86
Sanderling	*Calidris alba*	38
Sandpiper, Buff-breasted	*Tryngites subruficollis*	116
Common	*Actitis hypoleucos*	38,52
Curlew	*Calidris ferruginea*	38
Green	*Tringa ochropus*	52
Wood	*Tringa glareola*	52
Shelduck	*Tadorna tadorna*	4,23,opp *33*,38, 52,116
Shoveler	*Anas clypeata*	116
Shrike, Red-backed	*Lanius collurio*	109
Skylark	*Eremophila alpestris*	52,85,86,*93*
Smew	*Mergus albellus*	116,*123*
Snipe	*Gallinago gallinago*	opp *113*,122
Sparrow, House	*Passer domesticus*	132,*138*
Sparrowhawk	*Accipter nisus*	69
Spoonbill	*Platalea leucorodia*	*18*
Starling	*Sturnus vulgaris*	86
Stilt, Black-winged	*Himantopus himantopus*	37
Stint, Little	*Calidris minuta*	38
Stonechat	*Saxicola torquata*	53,109
Stone-curlew	*Burhinus oedicnemus*	98,*101*
Swallow	*Hirundo rustica*	53,110,132
Swan, Bewick's	*Cygnus columbianus*	116
Mute	*Cygnus olor*	116
Swift	*Apus apus*	132
Teal	*Anas crecca*	38,116
Tern, Common	*Sterna hirundo*	25,opp *33*,115, 117
Gull-billed	*Gelochelidion nilotica*	115
Little	*Sterna albifrons*	*25,25,31*,115
Tit, Blue	*Parus caeruleus*	85,133
Great	*Parus major*	133
Thrush, Song	*Turdus philomelus*	85
Turnstone	*Arenaria interpres*	38
Twite	*Carduelis flavirostris*	23
Warbler, Reed	*Acrocephalus scirpaceus*	52
Whitethroat	*Sylvia communis*	68
Wigeon	*Anas penelope*	38,116
Woodcock	*Scolopax rusticola*	68
Woodpecker, Green	*Picus viridis*	70,88
Great Spotted	*Dendrocopos major*	*76*
Woodpigeon	*Columba palumbus*	85,86,87
Wren	*Troglodytes troglodytes*	85
Wryneck	*Jynx torquilla*	68
Yellowhammer	*Emberiza citrinella*	85

3. FISH, AMPHIBIANS & REPTILES

Five native amphibia and four native reptiles breed in Essex. At least 23 species of fish breed in rivers and streams, including some introductions. Over 80 species of marine fish have been found in the Thames estuary. Laver (1898) is the most recent book to deal with the complete group. The Essex Biological Records Centre publication (1983) gives recent distribution maps for the reptiles and amphibia. A new work on the fish is in preparation (Wheeler); meanwhile the reports by the Anglian and Thames Water Authorities are the best source of information on Essex fish in recent times.

Species	Scientific name	Page refs.
Adder	*Vipera berus*	51,109,*112*
Bream	*Abramis brama*	119
Butterfish	*Pholis gunnellus*	*39*
Carp	*Cyprinus carpio*	119
Chubb	*Leuciscus cephalus*	119
Cod	*Gadus morrhua*	*39*
Dab	*Limanda limanda*	38
Dace	*Leucistus leucistus*	119
Eel	*Anguilla anguilla*	119,120
Flounder	*Platichthys flesus*	38
Frog	*Rana temporaria*	122,*138*
Goby, Common	*Pomatoschistus microps*	22
Rock		*39*
Grass-snake	*Natrix natrix*	122,*128*
Gudgeon	*Gobio gobio*	119
Guppy	*Lebistes reticulatus*	120
Lizard, Common	*Lacerta vivipara*	106,109
Loach, Stone	*Noemacheilus barbatulus*	119

Mackerel	*Scomber scombrus*	39		Rudd	*Scardinius erythrophthalmus*	119
Miller's Thumb	*Cottus gobio*	119		Ruffe	*Gymnocephalus cernua*	119
Minnow	*Phoxinus phoxinus*	119		Roach	*Rutilus rutilus*	119
Mullet, Red	*Mullus surmuletus*	39		Slow-worm	*Anguis fragilis*	109
Newt, Common	*Triturus vulgaris*	*121,122,147*		Sole	*Solea solea*	38
Great Crested	*Triturus cristatus*	*121,123*		Sprat	*Sprattus sprattus*	39
Palmate	*Triturus helveticus*	*121,123*		Stickleback, 3-spined	*Gasterosteus aculeatus*	*39*,119
Perch	*Perca fluviatilis*	119		Tench	*Tinca tinca*	119
Pike	*Esox lucius*	119,*128*		Toad	*Bufo bufo*	*76,123*
Pipe-fish, Great	*Syngnathus acus*	39		Trout, Brown	*Salmo trutta*	119
Worm	*Nerophis lumbriciformis*	39		Whiting	*Merlangius merlangus*	39
Plaice	*Pleuronectes platessa*	38		Wrasse, Corkwing	*Crenilabrus melops*	*39*

4. BUTTERFLIES AND MOTHS

Of the 58 species of butterfly that have been recorded in Essex 47 are known to have had resident populations at some time since the middle of the last century. 18 of these species are now extinct as breeding species, although some of these are still seen as rare vagrants. In addition there are 11 species which are migrants or vagrants to the county and have never had a resident population. The 1709 moth species (657 of the larger 'macro' moths and 1052 'micros') have suffered a much lower rate of decline than the butterflies. The butterflies and larger moths are covered by Firmin *et al* (1975) and this checklist will be brought up to date by a new publication late in 1984 (Emmet and Pyman). The smaller moths are dealt with by Emmet (1981).

Species	Scientific name	Page refs.		Species	Scientific name	Page refs.
Admiral, White	*Ladoga camilla*	69,72		Hairstreak, Brown	*Thecla betulae*	69
Beauty, Brindled	*Lycia hirtaria*	134		Green	*Callophrys rubi*	*opp 129*
Blue, Adonis	*Lysandra bellargus*	97		Purple	*Quercusia quercus*	*77*
Chalk-hill	*Lysandra coridon*	97		White-letter	*Strymonidia w-album*	*opp 129*
Common	*Polyommatus icarus*	52,106,*113*		Hawkmoth, Elephant	*Deilephila elphenor*	*139*
Mazarine	*Cyaniris semiargus*	97		Lime	*Mimas tiliae*	134,*139*
Silver-studded	*Plebejus argus*	100		Poplar	*Laothoe populi*	134,*135*
Brimstone butterfly	*Gonepteryx rhamni*	98,*102*		Privet	*Sphinx ligustri*	132
Brown, Meadow	*Maniola jurtina*	52		Lackey	*Malacosoma neustria*	24
Brown-tail	*Euproctis chrysorrhoea*	49,*57*		Ground	*Malacosoma castrensis*	24
Burnet, Narrow-bordered				Luffia	*Luffia ferchaultella*	110
Five-spot	*Zygaena lonicerae*	106		Orange, Frosted	*Gortyna flavago*	50
Six-spot	*Zygaena filipendulae*	106		Orange-tip	*Anthocharis cardamines*	*opp 128*
Carpet, Chalk	*Scotopteryx bipunctaria*	100		Peacock	*Inachis io*	*opp 128*,135
Copper, Small	*Lycaena phlaes*	*opp 128*		Peppered Moth	*Biston betularia*	134,*138*
Eggar, Small	*Eriogaster lanestris*	49		Puss Moth	*Cerura vinula*	134,*139*
Emerald, Essex	*Thetidia smaragdaria*	24		Ringlet	*Aphantopus hyperantus*	*77*,106
Emperor, Moth	*Saturnia pavonia*	*113*		Rosy Marbled	*Elaphria venustula*	109
Emperor, Purple	*Apatura iris*	69,*opp 129*		Satin, White	*Leucoma salicis*	134
Estuarine, Fisher's	*Gortyna borelii*	50,58		Skipper, Essex	*Thymelicus lineola*	52,*57,opp 128*
Fritillary, Dark Green	*Argynnis aglaja*	69		Grizzled	*Pyrgus malvae*	*113*
Duke-of-Burgundy	*Hamearis lucina*	69		Silver-spotted	*Hesperia comma*	97
Heath	*Mellicta athalia*	69,*opp 129*		Sycamore Moth	*Acronicta aceris*	*139*
High Brown	*Argynnis adippe*	69		Tiger, Cream-spot	*Arctia villica*	52
Pearl-bordered	*Boloria euphrosyne*	69,*77*		Garden	*Arctia caja*	132,*139*
Silver-washed	*Argynnis paphia*	69,*opp 129*		Tortoiseshell, Small	*Aglais urticae*	135
Small Pearl-bordered	*Boloria selene*	69		Underwing, Red	*Catocala nupta*	134
Gatekeeper	*Pyronia tithonus*	106,*opp 128*		Yellowtail Moth	*Euproctis similis*	*138*
Ghost Moth	*Hepialus humuli*	93		White, Marbled	*Melanargia galathea*	52,*opp 129*
Grayling	*Hipparchia semele*	109,*130*		Wood, Speckled	*Pararge aegeria*	69,*opp 128*

5. INSECTS OTHER THAN BUTTERFLIES & MOTHS

There are no complete county listings for any of these major groups of insects. Hammond (1979) gives a comprehensive listing of beetles for the Epping Forest area. Benton (1982) has given some information on dragonflies and damselflies and the same author is working on a full-scale publication on these insects.

Species	Scientific name	Page refs.		Species	Scientific name	Page refs.
Ant, Red	*Lasius flavus*	88,95		White-legged	*Platycnemis pennipes*	122
Beetle, Elm Bark	*Scolytus scolytus*	70		Scarce Emerald	*Lestes dryas*	52,*57*
Great Silver Water	*Hydrous piceus*	52		Dragonfly, Broad-tailed		
Stag	*Lucanus cervus*	70		Chaser	*Libellula depressa*	122,*129*
Bush-cricket, Great Green	*Tettigonia viridissima*	58		Ruddy Darter	*Sympetrum sanguineum*	*128*
Roessel's	*Metrioptera roeselii*	52,58		Glow-worm	*Lampyris noctiluca*	*102*
Cone-head, Short-winged	*Conocephalus dorsalis*	52		Mayfly, Anglers Curse	*Caenis* sp	*128*
Damselfly, Banded				Large	*Ephemera* sp	*128*
Demoiselle	*Calopteryx splendens*	*128*		Mosquito,		
Common Blue	*Enallagma cyathigerum*	*opp 113*,122		Orthopodomyia	*Orthopodomyia pulcripalpis*	64
Blue-tailed	*Ischnura elegans*	*opp 113*		Woodwasp, Giant	*Urocerus gigas*	*77*
Dainty	*Coenagrion scitulum*	52				

6. INVERTEBRATES OTHER THAN INSECTS

There are no complete listings of the Essex fauna for any of these groups. Davis (1967) and Barnes & Coughlan (1971) give very detailed records of the marine invertebrates of the Blackwater estuary.

Species	Scientific name	Page refs.
Barnacle (Elminius)	Elminius modestus	40
Brittle-star	Ophiothrix fragilis	39
Cockle	Cardium edule	25,37
Corophium	Corophium volutator	36,37
Crab, Shore	Carcinus maenas	22,32,40
Spider	Hyas araneus	39
Hydrobia	Hydrobia ulvae	36,37,45
Limpet, Slipper	Crepidula fornicata	40
Lobster	Homarus vulgaris	40
Lugworm	Arenicola marina	37,44
Jellyfish	Aurelia aurita	40
Macoma	Macoma balthica	37
Mussel	Mytilus edulis	37
Nereis	Nereis spp	37
Nephthys	Nephthys spp	37
Whelk, Fossil	Neptunia contraria	48

Species	Scientific name	Page refs.
Oyster	Ostrea edulis	39,40
American	Ostrea virginica	40
Portuguese	Ostrea angulata	40
Oyster-drill, American	Urosalpinx cinerea	40
Sabellaria	Sabellaria spinulosa	40
Sea-gooseberry	Pleurobrachia pileus	40,44
Sea-slater	Ligia oceanica	45
Shrimp, Brown	Crangon vulgaris	40
Pink	Pandalus montagui	40
Snail, Garden	Helix aspersa	103
Starfish	Asterias rubens	39
Sunstar	Solaster papposus	39
Tubifex	Tubifex tubifex	41
White-weed	Sertularia cupressina	41
Woodlouse, White	Platyarthrus hoffmannseggi	95

7. VASCULAR PLANTS (INCLUDES FERNS, FLOWERS, TREES & GRASSES)

The excellent Flora of Essex by Jermyn, published by ENT in 1974, recorded approximately 1375 species of vascular plants in Essex. About 915 were native species and the rest casuals, garden escapes or other types of human introductions. The figures are not exact as some plants (notably blackberries) have large numbers of micro-species most of which are not included in the tally. An additional 98 species are known to have once grown wild in Essex but to have become extinct since botanical recording began in the 19th century. More recent information on the rarest plants is given by Adams (1983) in which 98 species are listed as recently extinct or so rare that they feature in the 'red data' list of endangered species.

Species	Scientific name	Page refs.
Alder	Alnus glutinosa	59,66
Anemone, Wood	Anemone nemorosa	63,80
Arrow-grass, Sea	Triglochin maritima	22
Ash	Fraxinus excelsior	62,84
Aspen	Populus tremula	134
Aster, Sea	Aster tripolium	21
Beech	Fagus sylvatica	59,64,65,74
Beet, Sea	Beta vulgaris	25
Bindweed, Sea	Calystegia soldanella	25
Birch	Betula spp	65,74,109
Bluebell	Endymion non-scriptus	opp 49,63,75,79
Buckthorn, Purging	Rhamnus catharticus	98
Bracken	Pteridium aquilinum	108,109
Broom	Sarothamnus scoparius	109
Broomrape, Tall	Orobanche elatior	106,114
Campion, Red	Silene dioica	106
Sea	Silene maritima	25
Cannabis	Cannabis sativa	134
Chestnut, Sweet	Castanea sativa	61
Cleavers, Corn	Galium tricornutum	88
Clover, Sea	Trifolium squamosum	52
Sulphur	Trifolium ochroleucon	105,107,114
Clubmoss, Common	Lycopodium clavatum	113
Club-rush, Sea	Scirpus maritimus	52
Cord-grass, Common	Spartina anglica	21,22,31
Native	Spartina maritima	21,22
Smooth	Spartina alterniflora	22
Corn-cockle	Agrostemma githago	88
Cornflower	Centaurea cyanus	88
Cornsalad, Toothed	Valerianella dentata	88
Cowslip	Primula veris	62,88,103
Cow-wheat, Common	Melampyrum pratense	69
Crested	Melampyrum cristatum	102,105,107
Field	Melampyrum arvense	88
Crocus, English	Crocus purpureus	136
Crosswort	Cruciata laevipes	100
Daisy, Ox-eye	Leucanthemum vulgare	106
Dogwood	Swida sanguinea	97
Duckweed, Fat	Lemna gibba	52
Eel-grass	Zostera marina	36,41,44,50
Dwarf	Zostera noltii	36,44

Species	Scientific name	Page refs.
Elder	Sambucus niger	98
Elm	Ulmus spp	59,70,84,86,91
Wych	Ulmus glabra	70
Fennel, Hog's	Peucedanum officinale	50
Flax, Fairy	Linum catharticum	101
Fleawort, Field	Senecio integrifolius	98
Flowering Rush	Butomus umbellatus	129
Fluellen	Kickxia elatine	88
Fritillary, Snakeshead	Fritillaria meleagris	88
Fumitory, Narrow-leaved	Fumaria densiflora	98
Small Pink	Fumaria vaillantii	98
Small White	Fumaria parviflora	98
Glasswort, Common	Salicornia europaea	21,29,33
Branched	Salicornia ramosissima	47
Perennial	Salicornia perennis	22
Gorse	Ulex europaeus	108,109
Grass, Black	Alopecurus myosuroides	88
Borrer's Saltmarsh	Puccinellia fasciculata	52
Common Saltmarsh	Puccinellia maritima	21
Marram	Ammophila arenaria	25
Purple-stemmed Cat's-tail	Phleum phleoides	98
Squirrel-tail	Hordeum marinum	51
Guelder Rose	Viburnum opulus	103
Hare's-ear, Sickle-leaved	Bupleurum falcatum	105
Slender	Bupleurum tenuissimum	52
Hawthorn	Crataegus monogyna	49,83
Hazel	Corylus avellana	59,62,70,79
Heather, Bell	Erica cinerea	108,109
Heath, Cross-leaved	Erica tetralix	108
Hedge Parsley, Knotted	Torilis nodosa	51
Helleborine, Marsh	Epipactis palustris	100
Herb Paris	Paris quadrifolia	63,68,78
Hogweed	Heracleum spondylium	106
Hornbeam	Carpinus betulus	59,61,66,74,79,111
Ivy	Hedera helix	98
Kingcup	Caltha palustris	122
Knapweed, Greater	Centaurea scabiosa	106
Lily-of-the-valley	Convallaria majalis	63,79
Lime, Small-leaved	Tilia cordata	59,63
Common	Tilia x vulgaris	134

Ling	*Calluna vulgaris*	108	Primrose	*Primula vulgaris*	*opp 49*,62,63
Maple	*Acer campestre*	63	Purslane, Sea	*Halimione portulacoides*	22,*33*
Mayweed, Scentless	*Tripleurospermum inodorum*	88	Rattle, Yellow	*Rhinanthus minor*	88,122
Milk-vetch	*Astragalus glycyphyllos*	101	Reed, Common	*Phragmites communis*	52,54,55
Purple	*Astragalus danicus*	98	Rocket, Sea	*Cakile maritima*	25
Nettle, Stinging	*Urtica dioica*	98,135	Rockrose	*Helianthemum nummularium*	99
Oak	*Quercus* sp	59,60,64,65,66,	Saltwort	*Salsola kali*	25
		84	Sallow	*Salix* spp	59,134
Oat, Wild	*Avena fatua*	88	Saxifrage, Meadow	*Saxifrage granulata*	88
Orache, Hastate-leaved	*Atriplex hastata*	25	Scabious	*Knautia arvensis*	106
Orchid, Bee	*Ophrys apifera*	100,101,*107*,*opp*	Scurvy-grass, Danish	*Cheiranthus danica*	107
		112	Seablight, Annual	*Suaeda maritima*	21,*29*,47
Bird's Nest	*Neottia nidus-avis*	68,*78*,100	Shrubby	*Suaeda vera*	22,25,*33*
Early Purple	*Orchis mascula*	63	Sea-lavender	*Limonium vulgare*	22,*27*,*33*
Greater Butterfly	*Platanthera chlorantha*	63,68,*80*	Sea-holly	*Eryngium maritimum*	25,*32*
Green-winged	*Orchis morio*	88,*opp 112*	Sea-pink (See Thrift)		
Man	*Aceras anthropophorum*	100,*103*	Sorrel, Wood	*Oxalis acetosella*	63
Pyramidal	*Anacamptis pyramidalis*	100,105,106	Spurge, Laurel	*Daphne laureola*	*78*
Southern Marsh	*Dactylorhiza praetermissa*	100	Sea	*Euphorbia paralias*	25
Spotted	*Dactylorhiza fuchsii*	68,*73*,100	Sycamore	*Acer pseudoplatanus*	98
Oxlip	*Primula elatior*	*opp 49*,62,63	Tape-grass	*Vallisneria spiralis*	120
Pansy, Field	*Viola arvensis*	88	Tasselweed, Beaked	*Ruppia maritima*	52
Parsley, Cow	*Anthriscus sylvestris*	106	Spiral	*Ruppia cirrhosa*	52
Pasque Flower	*Pulsatilla vulgaris*	98,99	Thistle, Slender	*Carduus tenuiflorus*	51
Pimpernel, Scarlet	*Anagallis arvensis*	88,*opp 112*	Thrift	*Armeria maritima*	22
Pine, Scots	*Pinus sylvestris*	59,60,107	Thyme, Wild	*Thymus serpyllum*	99
Plantain, Sea	*Plantago maritima*	22	Tormentil	*Potentilla erecta*	109
Plane, London	*Platanus hybrida*	134	Trefoil, Slender Bird's-foot	*Trifolium micranthum*	52
Pondweed, Broad-leaved	*Potamogeton natans*	120	Twayblade	*Listera ovata*	100
Curled	*Potamogeton crispus*	120	Venus's Looking Glass	*Legousia hybrida*	98
Fennel	*Potamogeton pectinatus*	120	Violet	*Viola* spp	69
Perfoliate	*Potamogeton perfoliatus*	120	Water Crowfoot, Marine	*Ranunculus baudotii*	52
Shining	*Potamogeton lucens*	120	River	*Ranunculus fluitans*	120
Poplar, Hybrid Black	*Populus x euramericana*	134	Water-violet	*Hottonia palustris*	*129*
Poppy, Field	*Papaver rhoeas*	88	Wayfaring-tree	*Viburnum lantana*	97
Long Prickly-headed	*Papaver argemone*	98	Willowherb, Great hairy	*Epilobium hirsutum*	106,*139*
Round-headed	*Papaver hybridum*	98	Wormwood, Sea	*Artemisia maritima*	22,24
Yellow-horned	*Glaucium flavum*	21,25,*opp 33*	Yellow-wort	*Blackstonia perfoliata*	105,*107*

8. NON-VASCULAR PLANTS (ALGAE, LIVERWORTS, MOSSES, FUNGI)

Mosses and liverworts have a detailed section by Dr Adams in the *Flora of Essex* (Jermyn, 1974). The marine algae of Essex are listed in Milligan (1965) but there is no similar list for the fresh-water species. Swale & Belcher (1959, 1964) give details of the algae in the River Lea and the Charophyte algae are dealt with in the *Flora of Essex*. Although there is no list of Essex fungi, several have been published for the Epping Forest region. The most recent is Boardman, Wilberforce & Ward (1970) although studies since then have rendered this well out of date.

Species	Scientific name	Page refs.			
Agaric, Fly	*Amanita muscaria*	70	Pond algae	*Spirogyra*	*129*
Death-cap	*Amanita phalloides*	70	Polytrichum Moss	*Polytrichum* sp	*114*
Enteromorpha	*Enteromorpha intestinalis*	36	Sea-lettuce	*Ulva latuca*	36
Fungus, Birch Bracket	*Piptoporus betulinus*	70	Stink horn	*Phallus impudicus*	*80*
Honey	*Armillaria mellea*	70	Wrack, Bladder	*Fucus vesiculosus*	36
			Knotted	*Ascophyllum nodosum*	36

General Index

Note: Plant and animal species are indexed in the Species Index and are not included in this index. References to *illustrations* are in italics.

ENDPAPERS: Nature conservation sites in Essex. (Map prepared by DC on a base map drawn by KA.)

Postscript 1986

It is only eighteen months since I completed writing *The Nature of Essex* in the Silver Jubilee year of the Essex Naturalists' Trust. In adding this postscript, it is a pleasant duty to record my thanks to the readers of the first edition. Not only did they buy enough copies to permit a second edition, but many were kind enough to send me comments concerning sections of the book on which they had detailed knowledge. These comments have allowed me to correct at least some of the blunders which crept into the first edition. What I have not been able to do, is to completely rewrite each chapter to include events of the last eighteen months. So the main purpose of this postscript is to bring the story up-to-date.

Ancient, flower-rich meadows have featured prominently in the recent work of the Trust. A survey of the whereabouts and quality of each meadow in Essex has been completed and is the first step in the process of protecting, by purchase, the best of these meadows. So far, the Trust has bought three new meadow nature reserves; Oxley Meadow near Tiptree and Horndon Meadow in the Basildon district each have a colony of several hundred green-winged orchids, while Sweetings Meadow at Lindsell is best known for its pyramidal orchids.

Another orchid meadow, unfortunately not protected as a nature reserve, brought the Essex Naturalists' Trust and flower-conservation in general, to the national headlines in 1985. The orchid field on Mersea Island contained over fifteen thousand green-winged orchids — more than half the county's population of this rare species. There were also several other rare flower species. The owners of the field applied for planning permission to build houses on the land and, when they heard that the Nature Conservancy Council was applying for an order to protect the site, they sprayed weed-killer on the orchids at dead of night and under police protection. The national outcry at this act of legalised vandalism was one of the main reasons that the new Wildlife and the Countryside Act was amended so quickly. The loop-hole that permitted destruction of a proposed Site of Special Scientific Interest, while negotiations proceed, was closed. If these events were repeated today, the police would be protecting the orchids, not the land-owners.

The Mersea saga is far from over. The field is still the subject of a planning application, which has been considered by a public inquiry. Not all the flowers were destroyed, and it seems likely that the site will still merit listing as an SSSI when the present temporary protection runs out (and assuming that planning consent is refused). Within a year or so the Mersea orchid field will either be recovering from its sad experience or gone forever under a profitable housing development.

As well as accepting some amendments to the Wildlife & the Countryside Act, the Government has made a welcome increase in the funds available to the Nature Conservancy Council. This has permitted some speeding-up in the rate at which important sites in Essex can be re-notified, thus extending the protection of the news laws to them. There is still a long way to go. At the same time, the Government has encouraged a flood of proposals for major developments which threaten many of the remaining rural areas of Essex.

Attempts by conservationists to prevent the massive development of the Stansted area have failed. The Essex Naturalists' Trust is still involved in trying to influence the detailed planning decisions that follow from the Government choosing to destroy the region around Hatfield Forest for another airport.

The plans for a major drainage scheme in Constable country (see page 122) have been dropped, following protests by many organisations. The use of tin-based anti-fouling paints, which were poisoning marine life in estuaries (see page 40), is being phased out. These are two examples of battles where the Essex Naturalists' Trust has fought on the winning side.

Cambridgeshire County Council wishes to increase its road network as the development of East Anglia proceeds apace. Instead of making the A505 a dual carriageway, it has announced plans to blast a new road through the remote chalklands on the borders of Essex and Cambridgeshire. If it is built, this road will concrete over the last breeding sites of the stone curlew, which still nests in the area.

At the other end of the county, a consortium of private house-builders has got together to try to break the protection of green-belt land from building development. If they succeed, a major new town will bury a previously rural region in the Tillingham area.

In Colchester, an ancient woodland was threatened by another, smaller scale building plan. This planning application was rejected, due mainly to the Trust's vigorous campaign to protect one of the few ancient woodlands in the area. The battle of Bullock Wood was won, but the war is not over. After the planning decision was made, the wood was put up for sale. Before any conservation body or local authority could make a bid to save the wood, it was snapped up by a private individual for its development/investment potential. Clearly, someone thinks the existing protection can one day be broken.

As well as defending habitats from planning developments, the Trust has become increasingly involved in helping to enforce legislation which protects our rarest species. Badgers, despite the stricter laws, have suffered from an increase in the barbaric sports of badger-digging and baiting. The Trust's Essex Badger Protection Group has received splendid co-operation from the police, and there have been several successsful prosecutions of badger-diggers. The waste-disposal firm, Clean-away, who are proud of the badgers that live on the firm's works site at Pitsea, have made funds available to offer a reward, for information leading to the successful prosecution of badger diggers anywhere in Essex.

The Essex Bat Group has also been busy, and involves an increasing number of enthusiasts in the main work of persuading householders, and church authorities, to give their bats the protection that the law says they should have. One success story that I am especially glad to report concerns the bats of the Grays deneholes. On page 100 I wrote that naturalists had not visited the site for some twenty years. This has now been put to rights, and the Essex Bat Group has found that three species of bats are still using the deneholes as a hibernation site. Following helpful discussions between the Thurrock District Council, the Nature Conservancy Council and the Bat Group, access by pot-holers has been restricted during the winter season. The pot-holers are co-operating with the bat survey work, and there is already evidence that the number of bats using the holes is increasing, as the amount of human disturbance has declined.

The attempts to re-introduce the Heath Fritillary butterfly (see plate VIII) have succeeded. The butterfly is now breeding again in a woodland nature reserve 'somewhere in Essex'. Regrettably, it still seems necessary to keep the site a secret, to protect the butterflies from the attention of criminally inclined collectors. The heath fritillary has total legal protection, but so does the Essex emerald moth — a species that may have been exterminated in Essex by an unscrupulous collector. In 1985, at the nature reserve which was home to the last colony of this moth in Essex, all the foodplants were uprooted. This seems to have been done by a collector searching for the caterpillars. As a result, the species may be extinct in the county which gave it its name.

Any report on wildlife conservation is a mixture of success and failure. Two things encourage me to believe that, if I am ever lucky enough to revise the *Nature of Essex* for a third edition, there will be some good news to report. The first reason for optimism is the changing relationship between farmers and conservationists.

In recent years conservation bodies have often been involved in arguments with farmers and foresters about how rural areas should be managed. Recently, changing economic circumstances, and an increasing awareness by farmers of the need for public support, if state-aid for farming is to continue at a high level, have led to some *rapprochement*. The support that the farming community is giving to the Essex Farming & Wildlife Advisory Group, and a number of conservation initiatives (such as replanting lost hedgerows), is encouraging. There will still be arguments between farmers and conservationists. Equally often they are likely to be arguing on the same side: both in defence of rural land demanded by developers, and in asking the Government to restructure economic incentives, to help farmers with the conservation management of land they own or occupy.

The second reason for optimism concerns the Essex Naturalists' Trust itself. In its jubilee year, it realised the need to become a much more business-like operation if it is to succeed in protecting the wildlife of Essex for another twenty-five years. A small sign of this changed approach came when the Trust, with grant-aid from the Nature Conservancy Council and British Petroleum, took delivery of its first computer. The computer holds not just the business and membership records of the Trust but also helps record the details of the most important wildlife sites in Essex.

The Trust has constructed a plan of its priorities for the next few years. Top of the list is the purchase of new reserves, covering those habitats which are under-represented in the present list of protected areas: coastal marshes, flower-rich meadows and ancient woodlands. At the same time, the Trust, now a major land-owner, needs to spend money on equipment and manpower, to manage its existing nature reserves for the maximum benefit of wildlife.

The wildlife that exists in the 95% of the county that will never be a nature reserve, will depend on the attitudes of decision-makers and land-owners. The Trust will need to play an even more active role in campaigning for conservation in the wider countryside, and will also be turning its attention to the urban environments of Essex. In towns, quite small scale initiatives can make interesting wildlife habitats, and can involve and enthuse many people, especially the young, towards an enjoyment of wildlife.

The cost of making these plans succeed has been calculated: a minimum of £800,000 over the first five years. The Trust has launched an ambitious campaign to create an Essex Wildlife Action Fund, to ensure that money will be available for all these important plans. If, having read this postscript, you join the many people already actively involved in creating the fund, its success will be ensured.

164

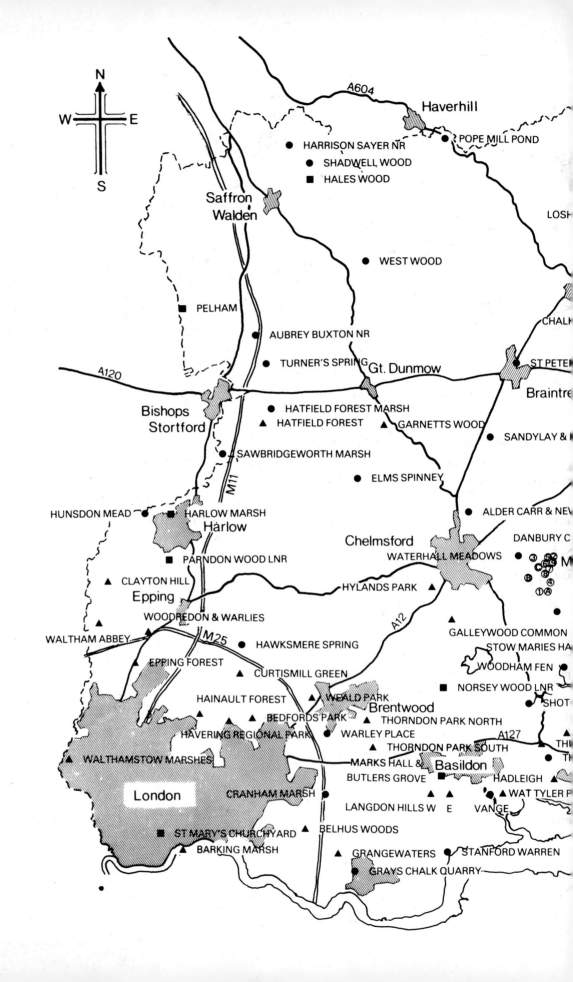